PORTSMOUTH
The Life of a Town

PORTSMOUTH

The Life of a Town

OLA ELIZABETH WINSLOW

THE MACMILLAN COMPANY, NEW YORK
COLLIER–MACMILLAN LIMITED, LONDON

The Macmillan Company, New York
Collier-Macmillan Canada, Ltd., Toronto, Ontario

Library of Congress catalog card number: 66–11111

Printed in the United States of America

Frontispiece: Portsmouth in Revolutionary Days. Courtesy of the New Hampshire Historical Society.

Acknowledgments

FOR THE illustrations in this book grateful acknowledgment is due to the following for permission to reproduce items from their collections:

New Hampshire Historical Society, Concord, N.H.— Portsmouth in Revolutionary Days; Garrison House in York, Maine; gundalow loaded with lumber; Fort William and Mary; Major Robert Rogers of the Rangers; *Ranger* receiving the salute to the Stars and Stripes, February 14, 1778; General John Stark; lightning rod put up by Benjamin Franklin on the Warner House

Portsmouth Historical Society, John Paul Jones House, Portsmouth—Bust of John Paul Jones by Jean Antoine Houdon; coat of arms of John Paul Jones; leather buckets in the John Paul Jones House; portions of the log pipe from Portsmouth's first water system

National Maritime Museum, Greenwich, England—Seafight of the *Bon Homme Richard* and the *Serapis* off Flamborough Head, September 23, 1779 (No. 210, photograph

ACKNOWLEDGMENTS

of line engraving by Lerpiniere and Fittler after R. Paton)

John Carter Brown Library, Brown University, Providence, R.I.—Captain John Smith's Map, in *A Description of New England,* London, 1614

The Boston Public Library—Vander Aa's lithograph of Pring's Harbor in James Hurly Pring's *Captaine Martin Pringe,* Plymouth, England, 1888

Society for the Preservation of New England Antiquities, Boston—The Jackson House

Portsmouth Public Library—The Olde Town Pump, in Helen Pearson and Harold H. Bennett's *Vignettes of Portsmouth,* 1913

Contents

Prologue

THE BEGINNING of every town in early New England is a story of adventure and the courage to meet it. No two towns began in exactly the same way. Boston began when Governor Winthrop and three other men stood under a "brave old Oake by the waterside" and agreed to form a church and to live together as the Bible taught them. Hartford, Connecticut, began when Thomas Hooker and his congregation walked a hundred and fifty miles through the wilderness, carrying their possessions on their backs and driving their cattle before them. They walked ten miles a day, milked their cows, and lived on the milk during their journey. Providence, Rhode Island, began when Roger Williams and four other men paddled a canoe across the Seekonk River and met a group of Indians on Slate Rock. "What cheer, Neetop?" Roger Williams called out. The Indians knew that this was a friendly greeting and they received the white men peaceably. The friendship that began on that rock lasted a lifetime. Portsmouth, New Hampshire, which is our story in this book, began when a young man discovered a river. His name was Martin Pring and he was twenty-three years old.

There is always a reason why a city stands where it is, and Martin Pring's discovery in 1603 is the reason Portsmouth stands at the mouth of the Piscataqua River. The word Piscataqua is an Indian name which means *where three rivers make one,* and that is exactly what happens at this point where three separate branches of this river come together and pour their waters into the Atlantic Ocean.

Where a city stands also determines many things in her history. In the early days of her first settlement Portsmouth had experiences like most other first towns' in the American wilderness. But because she is a seaport, she also had other experiences that could happen to no inland town. It was the river which made most of these differences. History— American history in this seaport town—began on that summer morning in 1603 when Martin Pring turned his little ship into the wide mouth of the Piscataqua, and sailed against its swift current. His discovery was the first chapter in a thrilling tale that is now more than three hundred years long.

∼1∼

Martin Pring Discovers the Piscataqua

MARTIN PRING lived in the days of great Queen Elizabeth, when sailing to the New World was every English boy's dream. He was one of the lucky ones who turned his dream into a page of history by making a discovery. Perhaps he was lucky to grow up in Devon, the home county of England's greatest seaman of his time, Sir Francis Drake. In fact, Martin was born in the very year that Sir Francis carried the English flag around the world for the first time. He had gone, with the secret permission of Queen Elizabeth, to capture Spanish ships on the high seas, and to bring home their cargoes of treasure. He did just that.

Every boy in England knew the story. He had set forth with five ships. Two had been abandoned. One had returned to England, and one was lost in a storm in the South Seas. But his flagship, the *Golden Hind,* sailed on alone, went the full length of South America, passed through the Strait of

Magellan, and dared the Pacific, widest of oceans. On the home stretch, it rounded the Cape of Good Hope at the southern tip of Africa, and arrived safely home in triumph at Plymouth, England, on September 26, 1580. Martin Pring was not yet a full year old.

From that day the *Golden Hind* was England's most famous ship and the inspiration of a thousand dreams. A whole generation of English boys grew up learning the ways of ships and sailing, while they waited for their chance to go. In port towns, Plymouth, Falmouth, Bristol, Southampton, London, they watched while ships were being built, rigged, launched, and sent off on their first voyage. They knew scores of ship names. They learned ship ways and ship talk. They were at home on the docks and in the warehouses, doing hundreds of ship chores and odd jobs on the wharves. They knew sailors, fishermen, merchants, and took every chance offered them to go out of sight of land in one kind of ship or another.

Martin Pring was one of those boys. He grew up in Devon, sharing the local pride in the great Sir Francis, whom he may even have seen. Among his boyhood tales were those of American Indians, men tall as giants, with paint on their faces, feathers in their hair, and arrows that never missed. During those years several Indians were brought to England, complete in their war paint and feathers. They danced their war dances, showed their skill with bows and arrows, and were better than the stories about them. When Martin was five years old, Sir Walter Raleigh made the first attempt to found a colony in what we now call Virginia. The colony

failed, but it had been a beginning and other attempts would
soon follow. All over England men began to talk of going to
America, just as men now talk of going out into space, maybe
to the moon.

Boyhood past, Martin went to Bristol, one of England's
busiest ports, a place of shipbuilding, of coastwise commerce,
of fishing fleets, and of expeditions setting off to the New
World. This city by the sea was one of the best places in
England to learn how to be a sailor. Years of hard work and
severe discipline taught Martin what he needed to know and
developed skills of many sorts. He saw how ships were made,
keel, spar, mast, boom, rigging. He learned weathers and
how to predict them, prevailing winds at every season, compass, sounding lines, islands, and danger zones. Perhaps most
eagerly of all, he read the record of explorations Englishmen
had made since John Cabot sailed out of Bristol in 1497,
discovered the coast of North America, and took possession in
the king's name. Many other expeditions had gone out of
Bristol, usually two or three ships under one commander.

Some were never heard of again. Some were forced to
return because of sickness on board or mutiny of the crew.
A few were successful. It was these that kept the boys dreaming, and inspired new hope in the young men ready to be
off. Word kept on coming back of treasures of gold, of
stores of fish that would make merchants the richest of men,
of giant masts for a thousand ships in the vast forests that
had no end. It seemed that the New World had everything
men could desire. Bristol was one of the gateways from
which to go.

PORTSMOUTH

Martin Pring's great chance came in 1603, when the mayor of Bristol and a group of leading merchants of the city chose him to command a voyage of exploration to the "northern part of Virginia," or New England, as we would say. For a young man only twenty-three this was a chance indeed, and it was also a compliment to both his character and his training. These Bristol merchants had been watching his progress through the years of hard work and early experience on the sea. He had used his time well and now he was ready to go.

Two ships were immediately fitted out for him, the *Speedwell,* of fifty tons, with a crew of thirty men and boys, and the *Discoverer,* of twenty-six tons, with a crew of thirteen men and one boy. Both ships could easily be tucked today into a corner of the hold in either the *Queen Mary* or the *United States.* Martin Pring's mate on the *Speedwell* was Edmund Jones. The Master of the *Discoverer* was William Browne and his mate was Samuel Kirkland. Among the sailors on the *Speedwell* there was a boy who was a musician and by a most happy chance he had brought his guitar along with him. It proved to be one of the most fortunate pieces of baggage on board. In off-duty hours through the long voyage this boy entertained the sailors, and in the New World he would entertain the Indians who came to visit the white men. The savages, Martin Pring wrote, took "great delight" in the boy's music, danced in a ring around him singing "lo la, lo la, lo la," and gave him many presents. He received tobacco pipes, tobacco, and what probably pleased him most of all, "snakes skinnes six foot long, which they use for girdles," or belts. He probably took home belts enough to last a lifetime.

There were two passengers on board of whom no work was required. These were two great English mastiffs, large, strong, and trained as watchdogs. We even know their names, Foole and Gallant. Foole had a trick. He could carry a pikestaff, or long pole with a prong in the end, in his mouth and keep it level as he ran. The sailors made a great deal of this trick, not knowing that the day would come when the Indians would not know that he was only playing. That day Foole would be a hero.

Both the *Speedwell* and the *Discoverer* were stocked with provisions for eight months, although Martin Pring hoped to return sooner. The food was standard ship fare for those days: mainly dried peas, salt beef, salt fish, cheese, beans, butter, and "good English Biskets," which we would call crackers. There might have been a few chickens on board, and maybe a goose or a pig, for even small ships carried them. The lack of fresh food, especially green vegetables and fruit, was one of the hardships sailors faced in 1603, and also one of the reasons a crew sometimes mutinied and demanded that the ship turn home again. But Martin Pring escaped this danger. His crew gave him no trouble. These men and boys, like himself, were glad for the chance to go.

His ships also carried trinkets as gifts and articles for sale or exchange with the Indians he hoped to meet. Both ships were stocked with bright-colored hats, green, blue, red, yellow; stockings, thimbles, pins and needles, looking glasses, beads, bells, bugles, scissors, toys, and, of course, axes, spades, saws, knives, hatchets, enough to sell as well as for their own use. Like most other early voyages of exploration, this one was a trading adventure as well as a chance for discovery. Merchant business for the future was the hope of the men who had fitted out these two ships and provided the articles for sale. Until the coming of the *Mayflower,* all exploration in America had also been largely in the hope of treasure, or of trade with articles secured from the Indians. The search for religious freedom would wait seventeen years longer, until the *Mayflower* sailed, bringing the Pilgrims to Plymouth in 1620.

Preparations completed, both ships sailed from Kingrode, Bristol, on March 20, 1603. If departure were as usual on such voyages, Captain Pring, his officers, and all his sailors would have gone to a special church service that morning, heard a sermon, taken solemn vows, and received a blessing before going on board. They knew the dangers and uncertainties ahead, as did the families and friends who attended the service with them and then gathered on the wharf to say good-bye.

The ships had hardly gotten started when contrary winds drove them back to Milford Haven, where they were becalmed for several days. Before a favoring wind came, news was brought on board that Queen Elizabeth had died. What would happen to England now? Of course no one could know that her death would mean the beginning of a quite new age in English history. But there was not much time even to wonder about England's future on the Milford Haven dock, for suddenly the winds came up again and both ships were off once more. Unless a faster ship overtook them, they would not know that James I was king of England until the long voyage was over and they were at home again.

Martin Pring sailed the direct route discovered by earlier navigators, taking him close to the Azores and saving crossing a thousand miles of sea. The lane for modern ocean liners follows this same course. He escaped severe storms, for this was summertime, but there were periods of calm sea and slow progress. It was not until June 7, more than two months since their feet had touched the solid earth, that land was sighted. The first sight of land must have been a triumphant moment for those forty-eight men and boys. It came, Martin Pring wrote, close to a "multitude of small islands" along the shore, probably what we now call the Isles of Shoals, along the Maine and New Hampshire coast. In those days the mainland had no special name, but was all a part of Virginia.

Martin Pring was not looking for islands and he merely mentioned this rocky group. Like all early explorers with the Atlantic behind them, he was looking for safe harbors and rivers that led far into the land. Rivers would be traffic lanes. They offered power to turn sawmills, and their bordering valleys were fertile fields in which the first settlers might grow food for survival. He was not looking for a place of immediate settlement, but was making a map which would guide later settlers. Maps came first. He was also looking for Indian camping grounds and a chance to establish the beginnings of trade.

As he came closer to the shore and coasted along, four rivers came into view on successive days. They looked hopeful. He would try them all. The Saco River came first, and seemed to offer a good harbor, but as he tried to explore it farther, he found the mouth too clogged for easy progress. The Kennebunk and York rivers similarly did not pierce far enough into the land at a depth hopeful for navigation, and therefore would not be useful for either navigation or trade. After these three disappointments, the discovery of the Piscataqua, which he called the "westermost river," and "a noble sheet of water," made it a memorable day. As he feared the *Speedwell* might prove too large for useful exploration beyond the river's wide mouth, he left it under guard at the harbor, and proceeded upward in the *Discoverer* with only a part of his crew. The deep channel and the swift current looked very promising.

There were anxious moments soon after leaving the wide mouth. Could even this small ship get through the Narrows? Yes, but not without some peril. Immediately afterward, the channel broadened, the currents became more swift, and the firm shoreline made landing easy. Captain Pring moored the ship and the whole party went ashore. As far as anyone knows, their feet were the first of any white men's to step on the New England mainland at this point.

At once they began the search for sassafras trees, one of the principal instructions from their Bristol sponsors. Sassafras is a native New England tree, and according to popular belief in Martin Pring's time, its root had great healing power. In the previous year, Bartholomew Gosnold, another explorer, had collected a large cargo of sassafras without first asking permission of Sir Walter Raleigh, who by authority of Queen Elizabeth had general charge over the whole territory of Virginia. When Gosnold announced his find, English customers swarmed upon it by the hundreds, the price dropped, and excitement increased. When Sir Walter heard of this frantic demand for sassafras, he was indignant because his permission to gather it had not been asked, and immediately he ordered all the unsold cargo to be destroyed. Martin Pring had heard of this order and the disappointment of the customers, and he had taken care to ask Sir Walter's permission before he sailed. It was promptly given. Unfortunately this more northern part of New England was the wrong place to find sassafras. Gosnold had found his abundant cargo farther south.

Unaware that his discovery of the Piscataqua River was worth far more than many shiploads of sassafras, Pring and his men turned southward after exploring the shore of the river for some twelve miles upstream. He had taken careful soundings all the way and charted the course of the river as far as he had gone. On the way down to the mouth he passed forests that seemed to have no end, the quiet waters of a great bay whose depth was a surprise, and several large islands near the mouth of the river. He and his men were disappointed in not finding any Indians, although the ashes of recent fires told that there had been Indians all along the shore shortly before. Their camping spots were now deserted. This was the fishing season for Indians, and they were camped along the ocean shore, but Martin Pring did not know that. June days were passing and he must move on if he were to find sassafras. The *Speedwell* and the *Dis-*

coverer turned out of the wide channel and sailed southward.

Both ships stopped next at what seventeen years later would become one of the most famous spots in all American history—Plymouth, of course, with its great rock, Plymouth Rock, which thousands of Americans come to see every summer. In 1603, this famous spot had no name. Martin Pring called it Whitson's Harbor, in honor of the mayor of Bristol, who had sent him on this voyage. This name would be forgotten. It was midsummer at this Cape Cod harbor in 1603, warm, with soft airs and starry nights, good weather for the work these men had to do. They also had a time schedule to keep. They were three thousand miles from home and winter storms would be too much for their small ships. They cut boughs, made temporary quarters, and went to work.

With shovels and hoes they cleared garden spots and planted the seeds they had brought to test the fertility of the soil. It was late for planting, but wheat, rye, oats, barley, peas, and beans sprouted promptly and in seven weeks gave good prospects for a crop. This corner of America would grow food for the settlers who would someday come. Best of all to these men's eyes, the woods immediately around the camp site yielded an abundance of sassafras and cedar. The sailors spent days cutting, trimming, and loading the cargo on the ships. By the end of July, the *Discoverer* could hold no more. Captain Pring decided that this smaller ship should sail first and the *Speedwell* wait for its cargo to be equally complete.

The small ship with its crew of thirteen men and one boy

took the breeze and sailed slowly away. One may be sure that no work was done that morning by the men and boys of the *Speedwell* who watched from the shore. Would it be better to be one of those sailing three thousand miles in that heavily loaded ship or one of the thirty men and boys left behind? The *Discoverer* was going home. The *Speedwell* was now the only English ship on the Plymouth part of the Atlantic seaboard. The small settlement seemed strangely empty as the men and boys went back to cutting sassafras and cedar. Cutting, tying, and loading it would take many days, and they missed their *Discoverer* comrades. Two ships are better than one on the shore of a vast new wilderness.

These thirty men and boys had already learned that the land had its dangers as well as the sea. Not only were there strange animals that came by night, wolves that howled in the distance, but also there were always Indians, many of them in this region. They seemed friendly, had called often on the white men, and could converse a little using the words they had learned from occasional white fishermen along the Plymouth coast. Invited to eat, they sampled the white men's food and liked it, especially the dried peas. They exchanged some of their corn for the trinkets the white men had brought and came back for more. The boy musician played his guitar and received tobacco pipes and snake skins in approval. Foole and Gallant were special attractions as long as they were tied, but the minute the dogs were free, not an Indian was left in camp. The white men remembered this.

As soon as the *Discoverer* had gone, Martin Pring had taken added precautions. Always he kept a larger guard on the *Speedwell* when the sailors were at work in the woods. The dogs were always tied at the camp in case a surprise attack should come. It came. One day just at noon, when the men in the woods were either asleep or resting from their morning's work, their axes quiet, the Indians came. Without making a sound, they surrounded the camp and shot arrows from all sides at once. Then at a signal, what Martin Pring called "seven score of savages" bounded out of the thicket and entirely encircled the small barricade. For a few minutes it looked as though they also intended to invade the ship.

Instantly the guard on board fired the small cannon to give the alarm to the men in the woods. Immediately also the dogs were let loose and Foole was given the long pikestaff. He took it and bounded after a huddle of Indians. The sailors in the woods heard the alarm, and with firearms in their hands, came in full number. The Indians ran, more afraid of the dogs than of the armed men. Not another arrow was loosed and almost as quickly as they had come, all Indians had vanished.

Later some of them came back and pretended it had all been a joke. They had meant no harm, they said. No one had been hurt on either side, but Captain Pring was not deceived. He did not invite the Indians to eat with them again and ordered a closer watch kept day and night. The story of this real or pretended attack was widely told in the homeland, and several years later, Gottfried, a Dutch navigator, hearing of it, made a fancy sketch of his imagined view of the scene in a book that he wrote. Quite obviously he knew nothing of the New England shore, where palmetto

PRING'S HARBOR, *an imaginary view by one who had never set foot on New England. He knew of Foole and Gallant, however, and let them identify the spot as the summer camp of Captain Martin Pring and his men in 1603.*

trees do not grow, or of Indians, but there is Foole with a staff in his mouth, ready to take orders to pursue them. Whether the Plymouth settlers had seen Gottfried's book with this picture we do not know, but wisely they brought dogs with them in 1620.

PORTSMOUTH

Early in August, probably the 8th or 9th, the *Speedwell* weighed anchor and set sail homeward. The Indians were watching, and whether to celebrate the white men's departure, or for some other Indian reason, they set fire to the woods around the camp of Pring and his men. Captain and crew looked back on a stretch of flame that laid the earth bare for many miles. This may be the strip which the Pilgrims found bare of great trees when they came seventeen years later. Very probably it was.

The homeward voyage was accomplished safely and on October 2, six months after their departure from Bristol, the *Speedwell* arrived back in Kingrode. There had been no man lost, no serious mishap, no disaster of any kind. Martin Pring had made a good record and had written his name very plainly in the long story of early American exploration. He gave the log of his journey to Richard Hakluyt, who had been one of his sponsors. Hakluyt published it in his great collection of early voyages which he called *Purchas his Pilgrims*. Martin Pring was the first explorer to put the Piscataqua River on a map and to record a description of the region through which it flowed. He had found the place where a city would stand.

He also brought back trophies of his experience which helped to make this place seem real to his readers. Among these was a birchbark canoe seventeen feet long and able to carry nine men standing upright. It weighed only sixty pounds. Hundreds of Englishmen came to see, and marveled. They also looked eagerly at the many smaller trophies: feathers of strange birds, snake skins, Indian wampum, grasses, nuts, seashells. Every sailor had his own collection and his own story of the New World. Hundreds of Englishmen heard these tales.

Captain Pring made a second voyage to America four years later, but not for exploration this time. He was sent in search of Captain Challons who had sailed toward the Atlantic coast and had not been heard from for many months. The search to find him was unsuccessful, and it was thought he had gone down with his ship and all on board.

Captain Pring made still later voyages for the East India Company, in command of a small fleet. He died in 1626 but he had lived long enough to know of the first settlement along the Piscataqua River which he had discovered and explored in his twenty-third year, and also of the Plymouth colony founded where he and his men had lived and worked through one summer season. There is only one first time, and in the story of Portsmouth, Martin Pring's name is on the first page.

✌2✌

Seven Men Come to Stay

TWENTY YEARS passed after Captain Pring's discovery of the Piscataqua River before the first settlers came. During these years, 1603 to 1623, many ships sailed past the river's wide mouth. They were English, French, Spanish, and Portuguese, but as far as we know, no one of them turned in, explored the channel, or charted the river's course, as Martin Pring had done. One of these English mariners, however, performed a real service. He was none other than Captain John Smith, who came in 1614, when he was only thirty-eight years old and not yet famous to the whole world.

Three London merchants had sent him with instructions to catch whales and to find a gold and copper mine they had heard about. Captain John knew nothing about catching whales or finding a mine, but he loved adventure, he wanted to see America again, and he came. The London merchants had fitted out two ships for him; he collected a company of sailors and fishermen and set sail. After two months the two ships landed at Monhegan Island, off the coast of what is now Maine, a spot already well known for its fishing banks. He made this island his headquarters.

After two months not a whale had been caught. No wonder. These men had no proper equipment, and they did not even know the kind of whales they were expected to catch. They wasted many precious days. Captain John wrote:

"We saw many, and spent much time in chasing them, but could not kill any."

Finding the gold and copper mine was another vain dream. They had no idea where even to look for it. Why not try our luck at fishing, Captain John said. The whole ocean is a fishpond.

They went to work hopefully. The ships had cargoes of salt for ballast. They used it to preserve the fish which they spread on the shore to dry. They also trapped small animals: mink, beaver, marten, and otter, all of them plentiful; and there were no game laws yet to prevent hunting in the summer. Everyone went to work, fishing with pole and line, salting the catch, hunting in the woods, and managing the traps.

That is, all but Captain John Smith. He was no fisherman or hunter, nor wished to be. He was an explorer, and he had come this long way again with the secret hope of discovering something about this new world that had not yet been reported. Leaving all but eight men of his party at the fishing banks, he took a small boat and with his companions sailed slowly down the coast from Penobscot Bay to Cape Cod. He had his drawing materials with him, and as he sailed, he made his famous map of this shoreline that is printed somewhere in the early pages of nearly every American history book to the present day.

"I have drawne a Map from point to point," he wrote, "Ile to Ile, and Harbour to Harbour, with the Soundings, Sands, Rocks and Landmarkes, as I passed close aboord the shore in a little Boat."

That is exactly what he did, and it was a most valuable service.

Very soon the nine men in the little boat came to the wide mouth of the Piscataqua. Here were the three inlets, just as Martin Pring had written. Captain John had read Pring's report, he recognized the river, and wrote in his notebook, "a safe harbour with a rocky shore." He did not sail inside the harbor as Martin Pring had done. Instead he looked closely at the group of small rocky islands across from the river's mouth, named them "Smith's Isles," and sailed on.

Day after day, as his boat went farther south, he turned into small bays and inlets, drawing them all carefully on his map. He met some Indians, did a little trading, and collected a few furs. In his *Description of New England,* which recorded this journey, he looked far beyond his own time and thought of the days when every little inlet would have its town—not trading posts only, but places where men and women would live with their children at home.

"No landlords to racke us with high rents," he wrote. "No struggle to get justice in the courts. Here every man may be master and owner of his own labour and land."

It was a vision of freedom, of hard work, and of the contentment a man may earn by it. He was practical enough to see that fishing would not be prosperous until the fishermen lived here the whole year through. They must not be summer residents only. Trading also must be a twelve-month business, not in summer only. Captain John wanted to live here himself.

"Could I have but meanes to transport a colonie, I would rather live here than anywhere," he wrote.

On his return to England, his report was published and widely read. All over England his tales of abundance of fish, of fox, of eagle, of bear, of deer, and especially of lobster, and his description of fruits no Englishman had ever tasted inspired many other voyages, as men came to see these marvels for themselves.

He presented his map to Prince Charles, asking him to give this bountiful land a name. "Call it New England," the prince answered.

Nine more springtimes and summers came, bringing more ships, more fishermen each year. All summer the ships were anchored in coves along the shore of the Piscataqua's wide mouth. But when winter came, all were gone. The whales and thousands of small fish had the ocean to themselves. The

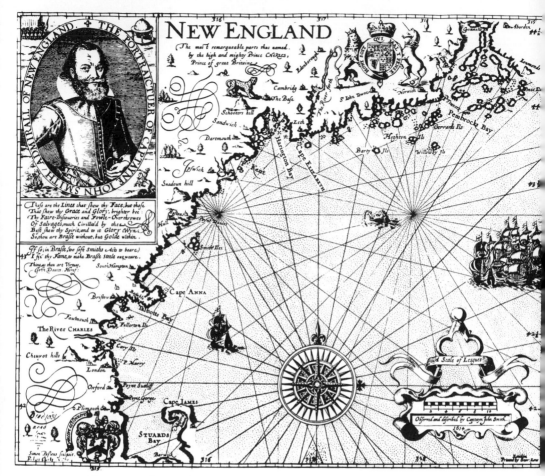

CAPTAIN JOHN SMITH'S MAP, *included in his* A Description of
New England, *London, 1614. The names he gave to coast points
are unfamiliar to us, but comparison of his coast line with later
maps shows a surprising accuracy of observation.*

fox, beaver, deer, and wolf claimed the land. Snow covered
all.

Farther down the Atlantic coast, in what we now call
Massachusetts, one hundred and one men, women, and

children landed in the winter of 1620 to begin the first permanent colony in New England. They had intended to go farther south, but they lost their way; their frail ship, the *Mayflower,* had cracked her main beam in mid-ocean, and when they first sighted land, they turned into what we now call Cape Cod Bay for shelter. They settled near the spot where Captain Pring and his men had lived through one summer seventeen years before. These new settlers called it Plymouth, in honor of the English port from which they had sailed. This was the name Captain John Smith had given it on his famous map, made in 1614. Fifty-one of these first colonists died during the first winter, but the other fifty built houses, cleared land, and stayed on. More ships from England brought provisions and, on each voyage, a few more passengers who also intended to stay. But these ships were bound for the struggling new settlement, and they sailed past the wide mouth of the Piscataqua, which was still empty until the summer fishing boats came back again, to anchor once more in the quiet coves along the shore.

But on a certain day of spring in 1623, another ship, also from Plymouth, England, did not sail past. It turned into the river's mouth, and went straight to the point called Panna-way on Little Harbor. The captain quite certainly knew where he was going. Very probably he had been here before. His ship was the *Jonathan* and David Thompson was the passenger who was coming to be the pioneer resident of this first settlement on the Piscataqua. He was a Scotsman, and had just received from the Plymouth Council a grant to six hundred acres of New England land at this point. He had also been given a grant to one island, wherever he might choose it. Two other men, whose names we do not know, were with him when he first arrived. These three men had agreed to stay during winters as well as summers, and to be the beginners of a permanent settlement of white men in this part of the New World. A month later another ship brought three more men who had made the same agreement. Still later a third ship brought two more. Seven men and their leader were to begin a settlement in the wilderness. Plymouth colony, their nearest neighbor to the southward, had numbered a hundred and one men and women three years earlier. Neither settlement now would be quite alone on this section of the coast.

Unlike that Plymouth company, these seven men and their leader had not come for religious liberty. They had come to fish, to trap small animals, and to trade with the Indians. The English merchants who had provided their passage, their food for the long voyage and for three months afterward, hoped to get rich from what a settlement in the New World would bring. These first men were to fish, dry their catch for shipment to England, and make a beginning of trade with the Indians. Like Captain Pring, they had brought trinkets, tools, and other small articles for sale or exchange. These would give them a start. After five years they would divide profits with the English merchants and the land would be theirs to keep.

Five years of stiff pioneering it would be, but these men were young and ambitious. Their leader was thirty-two. All were eager for adventure. Captain John Smith had been right. There were no landlords in this New World and there would be no rent to pay. Someday they would own their own land by their own labor. Five years seemed a short time for such a reward.

Building a house to live in was their first task. They cleared a space at the top of a hill that sloped down to the shore. Their small house crowning this gentle hill looked like a fort, as indeed it was intended to be. They built it of pine logs with a stone chimney put together with clay. The pines, the field stone, the clay were all near at hand. Pioneers use what they find, and what they do not find, they make. Pegs of oak are as good as nails, possibly better, and any man handy with a knife can make them. All early New England houses were pegged together. Birch bark is good for insulation and mortar made from native blue clay is excellent filling for the cracks. Guns were mounted within, at the sides of the house. There was a spring at the shore for a fresh water supply. The seven men had looked for that before they cut the first log.

Piscataqua House was the name by which they called it, although it was often called Pannaway, an Indian name for the point of the harbor where they had built it.

Except for David Thompson's wife, whom he sent for when the house was finished, and possibly a maid, there were no other women in this company at first. The seven men, their leader, and the two women lived together in the fort-like house. Other smaller houses were soon built, also a blacksmith shop, and storage sheds. A few Indians came by to trade. Occasionally a ship from home, bringing news, would leave a passenger who also had decided to stay, but usually these newcomers preferred to go on to Plymouth, where there was more companionship and the beginning of a more settled life.

One day in the late autumn of 1623, a visitor came from Plymouth. He was Miles Standish, the fiery little captain and military leader of Plymouth colony, a soldier brave far beyond his size, and one of the most useful men in the new settlement. When there was something difficult to do, Captain Standish was the man to do it. He had come to Pannaway on this occasion for provisions which his Plymouth people needed for the winter that was coming. Of course he got them. He also established a friendship with David Thompson, and invited him to make a return visit. What Miles Standish told him of the many small islands along the Cape Cod coast greatly interested David Thompson, who remembered that his grant entitled him to an island of his own choice. He would come later to see them. No, not now; there was work to do at Pannaway.

He and his seven companions soon found that Captain John Smith had been right when he said the whole ocean was a fishpond. They caught more fish than they could preserve with the salt that had come as ballast for the ship in which they had sailed. Very well, they would make salt out of the ocean, as they soon did. After many days of hard work, a "salt works" was set up on the shore. Small, of course, but it made "good salt" we are told. They also built fish flakes, or platforms on which to spread the fish for drying, on the hillside. Every inch of lumber for any purpose had to be cut, split, and pegged together. Every spoonful of salt took skill, labor, time. Those who came later would find everything easier. First settlers have the hard times.

Changes came even before the five years were over. When David Thompson went to Plymouth to repay the visit of Captain Miles Standish, he found an island that suited him. Thompson's Island it is still called. He lived for a short time on this island with his wife and small son, born at Pannaway. Then sickness came, as to so many in the Plymouth colony, and David Thompson died. This was a blow from which the small company at Pannaway could hardly recover. They were fishermen, unskilled in leadership, and they felt lost. They were almost too small a settlement to endure the loneliness, the monotony, and the dangers. But they stayed. Meanwhile a small group under two fishmongers, William and Edward Hilton, had come to a point farther up on the river, and they were nearer neighbors than the Plymouth people. In time the town of Dover would grow from this second small beginning. A few more settlers came to Pannaway. Fishing, hunting, trapping, and trading went on with only scant success. In spite of discouragements, however, these young men stayed.

Every fishing vessel that anchored in Little Harbor through these five summers took back a report of these men who lived at Pannaway in Piscataqua House. The name Piscataqua was now known to hundreds in England, who had heard of this comfortable house, the great fireplace, the Indian corn growing in the garden patch, the birds no Englishman had ever seen, the nets full of fish from the day's catch, the vast forests stretching all around. Scores of summer fishermen had told these tales to hundreds of listeners in the coast towns of England. Men and boys who listened wanted to come. There was magic in the very name of New England. Tales from the Plymouth settlement had traveled far also, and John Winthrop's company of more than a thousand men and women would soon sail in their seventeen ships to found Boston and to become the Massachusetts Bay colony to which hundreds more would soon come. The American dream was beginning to take shape in the hearts of Englishmen. It was not the dream of warriors, swords in hand, but of peaceful men and women who wanted to build new homes and be free to develop in their own way.

These first seven men at Pannaway, those who had come to join them later, and the newer small company up the river at Dover had done much more by staying through these first hard years than by catching fish and trapping animals. They had proved that no one need be afraid of New England winters. They had learned how to make fur caps and leggings for winter wear, how to preserve and store their food, and how to live in comfort and with pleasure in their small house on the hill. They had been pioneers and had opened the way to life throughout the year in this northern corner of the New World.

News of the next chapter for the Piscataqua region came unexpectedly. The first fishing boats in the spring of 1629 brought word that preparations were in progress for a new and larger settlement only two miles up the coast from Pannaway.

～3～

Strawbery Banke Is Settled

JOHN MASON was the man who was planning this new settlement. He was an Englishman, the former governor of Newfoundland. During his six years as governor of this northern island, he had learned many things about the Atlantic coast and had become interested in founding a colony there. He was already a man of wealth, but he believed the tales which were being told of great treasure in America and he dreamed of being a much richer man. He planned to bring over a small colony of men to work for him in finding some of this fabled treasure. He first made a personal survey of Newfoundland from shore to shore, but decided that this island was too far north and had too cold a climate for twelve-month residence and profitable labor. He read Martin Pring's account of the Piscataqua River, followed the reports of the men at Pannaway, and decided that the region around the mouth of the Piscataqua River was the place to found his colony.

When his six years as governor were over, he returned to

his home in Hampshire County, England, where he owned a large estate which he called Portsmouth. He made careful plans for his venture in America. First, in 1629, together with his friend, Ferdinando Gorges, he secured from the Plymouth Company a grant of six thousand acres in the Piscataqua region. This grant gave the two men an area extending from the Merrimack River to the Sagadahock, and as far back as the Great Lakes and the border rivers of Canada. All islands three miles from the shore were also included. A vast, unexplored area it was, larger than either man knew, larger even than the king or the Plymouth Company knew, but it would be none too large for the colony John Mason had in mind. He secured, also, partial control of the Pannaway region, which had been without supervision since David Thompson's death.

His plan provided for the sending over of forty-eight men and twenty-two women, all English, and eight Danes who would begin the settlement. Walter Neale, a former soldier, would be governor until John Mason could come over to take charge of the colony in person. Ten other men, called stewards, would act as foremen in directing the work of the men in the colony. This settlement was not, in the beginning, a company of free men and women who would buy their own house lots, have deeds for them, and own the houses they would build, as first settlers were doing elsewhere in New England. John Mason and Ferdinando Gorges were the owners of the Piscataqua settlement. They paid the passage of the men and women whom they sent over, and they would continue to supply everything needed, shelter, food, clothing. In return the tenants agreed to work for their masters under the direction of the ten stewards. This was a system well understood in England, and in the beginning, it was willingly accepted by the men and women who were to begin this new colony.

Two ships, the *Pide-Cowe* and the *Warwick,* brought the passengers over, but not all at the same time. Walter Neale, the appointed governor, came with a small group in 1630 and took up residence in Piscataqua House at Pannaway. He was agent for the company still concerned with Pannaway trade, and his first duty was to send them a cargo of beaver skins. His first duty for John Mason was to attempt to locate gold mines he had heard were somewhere in this region. The beaver skins were sent, but finding the gold mines was another story. Walter Neale set out with two companions in search, walking as far as what we now call the White Mountains. Their food gave out before the three men reached the top of the first range and they turned back discouraged. All they had found were a few clear pebbles, which they called crystals. They sent these to John Mason as samples, and named the mountains the Crystal Hills, a name that was forgotten long ago.

Humphrey Chadbourne and his fellow carpenters made a more hopeful beginning, as they began to build Great House, which would be the center of the settlement. They chose as a site, not the Pannaway region, but a spot two miles distant, on the shore of the Piscataqua River, looking north from the entrance to the harbor. It was a beauty spot indeed. The land they chose rises here from the water's edge up a long low hill, which in 1630 was completely covered with wild strawberries. Strawbery Banke, these first men called it, and no other name could have been so appropriate. A sunny clearing it was, with acres of wild strawberries that for generations only the blackbirds, the noisy crows, and smaller birds of many colors, perhaps a few Indians, had picked. With the river in full view at the front and miles of woodlands behind it, it seemed an ideal spot, and Humphrey Chadbourne went to work at once.

Great House, as its name suggests, would be larger than the house at Pannaway. It would be built of pine, with a stone foundation and chimney. The stone and the pine were ready at hand, and Strawbery Banke became all at once a bustle of activity. Sounds never heard here before broke nature's silence of centuries and startled bird and beast. Strokes of the ax, the buzz of saws, the poundings of hammers, and voices of men at work lasted from dawn to sunset. In the good weather of summer and fall Great House took shape, and when the *Pide-Cowe* and the *Warwick* came again in the following spring, bringing tenants, supplies, and furnishings, Strawbery Banke had already begun to look like a settlement. A storehouse had been built, small houses for most of the tenants, a shelter for cows and sheep; all were ready. Wells had been dug, and a blacksmith shop was in prospect. On the edge of the woods was a sawmill and along the shore, platforms for drying the fish. The men at Pannaway had given many hints as to the salting and preserving of the fish, which were abundant past imagining.

One of the most important of the early buildings was a

small fort at the outer entrance of the harbor. Four small cannons brought over by the first ship were installed and a guard was always kept on watch. Life at Strawbery Banke in these first years was mainly peaceful and clear of danger except from wolves that howled by night, but this small fort in plain sight from Great House gave the little settlement a sense of protection which was important. These eighty men and women must be ready at all times for whatever alarms these lonely shores might bring. Later a fortified house, called Garrison House, was built within the village, and a drumbeat at any hour called everyone to assemble there at once.

Indians were, of course, always a possible danger, but for many years they came only in friendliness. They brought furs to exchange for trinkets, pans, knives, bright-colored hats, beads, pins, needles, bells, toys, and other small articles of English manufacture. Every ship brought a fresh supply, but there was never enough to satisfy the Indian customers. Nor could the English merchants ever get enough beaver, mink, and marten skins to satisfy their London customers.

Hunting, trapping, fishing, preparing fish and furs for shipping were the principal occupations, as each season brought its special duties. With each, skill came with practice, but there was always more to do than daylight hours permitted. John Mason was slow to give up the hope of sudden wealth by the discovery of gold and silver, and he instructed the stewards to keep some of the men digging in hope of finding one or the other. They found only iron,

A GARRISON HOUSE *in York, Maine. Similar houses were once familiar in Portsmouth and other New England towns. Strongly built, fortified, and guarded, they were family citadels of defense against Indian attack.*

and that only after long labor, and not in great quantity. John Mason would have been far wiser if he had set them to work clearing many acres of land immediately and beginning an extensive cultivation of the soil. A company this size could have planted a crop and reaped a considerable harvest before even the first winter. Instead he insisted only on their setting out a small vineyard before even testing the soil for the raising of grapes for a wine supply. He kept sending meal for their bread, and expecting them to dig for gold and silver instead of growing wheat and corn. When supplies were low, he sent large cargoes. The wisest provision he sent was twenty-four cattle of a large yellow breed from Denmark, which meant milk and butter and cheese for the table, and very soon not only was there a profitable increase in the herd itself, but also a new stimulus toward the growing of wheat, oats, and rye for hay and grain. A shipment of seven hundred barrels of corn in one cargo showed John Mason to be a man of great generosity, but in no sense a pioneer. He was a city man, eager for greater wealth, but without the vision for a self-supporting colony.

He provided for the pleasure of these men and women who worked for him, as well as for their necessities—not only food and military equipment, but musical instruments for the entertainment of indoor winter days. Song and dance were pleasures of all ranks of English society in those days and one may imagine that the large room on the first floor of Great House was often a scene of merriment when the day's work was over. He also provided for their tables pewter dishes instead of wooden ones, more than a thousand of them. A more practical cargo for pioneers might have been far different, but such extras suggest that these early tenants were not only made comfortable, but that they also had hints of elegance in their daily living. U. S. 1358004

Now and then excitement came, and doubtless oftener

than we know. One such excitement, that came sooner or later to every coastal town, was pirates. They were in all waters. Their ships were swift and their sailors skillful. Usually their attacks came on the high seas. They overtook a merchant ship whose cargo they wanted, put the captain in chains, forced his sailors to take the ship where they pleased, sold the cargo, and escaped from pursuit. They also knew every seaport where furs, tobacco, rugs, and blankets were stored, ready for shipment. In 1632, the first year of residence for the colony on Strawbery Banke, Dixey Bull, an English pirate, put them in terror. He had come by night to Pemaquid, a small fishing harbor immediately north, and stolen furs, coats, and blankets stored for safety until the next ship came. The entire work of the season was gone. Swiftly a messenger hastened to Strawbery Banke to give the alarm and ask for help. As he hurried on to Boston to get more help, Governor Neale assembled forty of the Strawbery Banke men, equipped them with food and fire-arms, and with the twenty more men from Boston, hurried to Pemaquid in six small boats. They were just too late to catch Dixey Bull, who had escaped with his plunder. No one knew which direction he had taken. As the sixty men turned south again, suddenly the winds died down and for three weeks they were trapped in Pemaquid. What might be happening at Strawbery Banke? Nothing disastrous, fortunately. Dixey Bull never returned, for on his return to England with his stolen goods, he was arrested and executed at Wapping. The waterfront was always the place where the scaffold of a pirate was set up. When the scaffold falls, let the waves bear him away with it.

In 1634, when Strawbery Banke was four years old, Ferdinando Gorges sold his share of the grant to John Mason, who became the sole owner. Immediately he made plans to come over and take personal charge of the colony. He would call the whole grant New Hampshire, in honor of his own birthplace in Hampshire County, England. He would live in Great House. Maybe he could still find the gold no one had yet discovered.

But he was not to have that chance. In 1635, just as his plans were completed and he was ready to sail, he became suddenly ill and died. News of his death reached Strawbery Banke by the first boat, two months later. Confusion followed. The little colony was frail and struggling. Walter Neale had left the year before. The settlers needed above all else the energy and enthusiasm of a vigorous leader, and now John Mason was gone. There was as yet no settled minister who might have guided them as a temporary leader, as in Massachusetts towns. They had no plan of government. John Mason's widow was appealed to, but she sent back word that she would do nothing to supply the needs of the settlement. They felt lost.

Without either a leader or a plan of government, it was at first every man for himself. Several of the stewards left immediately, taking whatever they could carry with them. Two stewards drove one hundred of the yellow cattle to Boston and sold them for twenty pounds a head, keeping the money. A number of the other animals, the sheep, the goats, and the horses, were also sold by bolder ones among the workers. Some of the original forty-eight workers left, taking tools and supplies with them. Others decided to stay and claimed the small houses in which they had lived as their own. Everyone raided the storehouse until nothing was left, not even meal for their bread. It was midwinter soon and there was sharp distress. Appealed to for help once again, John Mason's wife said no. She would do nothing. It looked for a time as though an end had come to orderly life on Strawbery Banke, perhaps an end to life itself.

But that was not to be so. When the first confusion had died down, the settlers who had decided to stay, some of them stewards and some workers, met together and tried to face the future calmly. What did they do first? They did exactly what people who intend to live together in peace have done times without number. They made what they called a Combination. The Pilgrims on board the *Mayflower* had called it a Compact. The name does not matter. It was an agreement by which each man promised to act not for himself alone, but as one member of a group. The whole company would talk together in a meeting, take a vote, and whatever the greatest number wanted would be done. The Combination was a simple agreement to consult together and to act for the good of the whole. To this agreement each man signed his name. If he did not know how to write, and many of these men did not, he made a mark, and this was his vote. Orderly government and peaceable living begin in just such a simple promise.

Three men were chosen leaders; Francis Williams was called governor, but he would not give orders. He was only the chairman of the meeting. Ambrose Gibbins and Thomas Warrenton were his assistants. Every man in the group had as much right to speak and make suggestions as these three leaders. Each man's signature or his mark made him equal to any other man who had made the same promise.

We do not know the step-by-step story of what this small company decided during the first weeks and months of their experiment in self-rule. Very probably there were stormy times when agreement seemed impossible. Perhaps sharp quarrels came also. No doubt there were some members who in spite of having signed the agreement were often sulky and stubborn. It is always so. Town books of other first settlements report many uneasy times in their early records, sometimes even bodily injury when a stormy dispute was going on. Unfortunately the first record of Strawbery Banke meetings was destroyed seventeen years later by the members themselves. In 1652 they voted to cross out of the earlier record what they did not approve and to begin a new book. Perhaps they crossed out the early quarrels they were ashamed of.

From the few items they left and from others recorded elsewhere we learn that in 1640 they had set aside fifty acres of land for a minister, and had already built a chapel on it and a parsonage. These first settlers were members of the Church of England, and this chapel would have been Episcopalian, as we say, not Congregational, as the early meeting-houses of Massachusetts became. We know also that earlier

THE OLDE TOWN PUMP
*that stood at the side of
the Parade, now Mar-
ket Square. This was not
the first town pump.*

than 1640, Strawbery Banke built a jail. By looking at other
early town books we may imagine that also they set up a
whipping post for punishment of minor offenses, and made
regulations on the use of the Town Pump, on keeping
wading places for the cattle clear of fences, and on making
shortcut paths to the chapel and to the pastures. In all towns
from the beginning there was provision against fire. Chimney
viewers must make sure that every new chimney was built

safely. Watchers took turns walking the streets by night to detect sudden danger or ill conduct. Protection against Indians, always a major fear, meant regular military drill for every man and boy in the town, and there was a penalty for not responding to the call of the drum. Each of these regulations and many more had meant a majority vote in town meeting, sometimes after long debate, and after the vote had been taken, obedience to the rule was expected from all.

If John Mason had lived to take personal charge of his plantation, as he wished, it would have taken longer for Strawbery Banke to become a town managing its own affairs. Life would have been more comfortable, of course, with a generous patron supplying all their needs and directing their work day by day. Portsmouth rightly honors John Mason as its founder and owes him a grateful memory. He had sent over the first settlers and protected them during the first hard years. But the day would have come when nothing but independence would have satisfied these same men and women.

Instead independence came suddenly, also at their own desire. It came on the day when a small group of those who had decided to stay in Strawbery Banke met together and faced the future. It came when each man in his turn stepped up to the table, took the quill pen in his hand, and slowly, perhaps awkwardly, wrote his name or made his mark on the paper which they called their Combination. At that hour Strawbery Banke became a small republic of free men. New chapters of freedom lay just ahead.

❦ 4 ❧

"Call Us Portsmouth"

By 1652 there were fifty families in Strawbery Banke. The parents in some of these families were children of the first settlers in 1631. They now had young children of their own. Others were new settlers who had come year by year. The town was full of children of all ages. Strawbery Banke was now crowded with houses and there were no strawberries to be found. Why keep the old name? "Call us Portsmouth," said the town meeting in 1652. It is "a name suitable for this place. We are at the river's mouth, and our port is as good as any in the land." The General Court of Boston heard the petition favorably, and Strawbery Banke became Portsmouth.

This was the name John Mason himself had chosen more than twenty years earlier and it would not be changed again. With the new name came a new chapter of life on the Piscataqua. Twenty years had brought many changes in all of New England and Portsmouth would increasingly have a share in them. The remoteness and loneliness of the earliest years were gone. There were now more neighbors close by and more coming with each springtime. The years from 1635 to 1640 had been peak years of immigration and new settlers had come to America by hundreds. They would still come. Boston now numbered several thousand. New towns had sprung up on three sides of Portsmouth, north, south, and west. Dover, Exeter, and Hampton had each made a Combination and become a small republic, managing its own affairs and choosing its own leaders, just as Portsmouth was doing.

The most important immediate event of the year 1652, when the petition for change of name was sent, was that the territory we now call New Hampshire, all of it, was annexed to Massachusetts colony. Massachusetts had wanted this to happen for years and had worked to bring it to pass. Her colonists were spreading out toward the north and wanted land on which to settle. She claimed that nearly all of New Hampshire land had been included in her original charter, and according to the vague wording of that charter she had been right. It had given her all the land as far as the Merrimack River and three miles beyond as her northern boundary. Fair enough, if the river had continued to flow east and west, as it does near the mouth. But a short distance from the mouth, it turns sharply north, so that three miles from the shore on the opposite side would give Massachusetts a very large part of what is now the state of New Hampshire. When the charter was written there was no map, and no one had as yet explored the course of the river far from its mouth. No wonder New Hampshire objected.

PORTSMOUTH

This same land had been granted to John Mason in 1629 and settled by the Strawbery Banke people in 1630. After John Mason's death his grandson, Robert Mason, claimed it, and continued to do so for another generation. There was trouble ahead on this issue for nearly a century. A line fence can make trouble if only ten feet are involved, but in this long-continued dispute, thousands of acres were in question. But the annexation to Massachusetts lasted for twenty-six years, and during this time the boundary line was not so important. Portsmouth, Dover, Exeter, and Hampton were all under the authority of Massachusetts.

In many ways this union was good. The four small northern settlements grew as Massachusetts grew, and new settlers pushed northward. Massachusetts government was well organized and all her towns followed the pattern. There would now be a schoolmaster for every town with fifty householders. Children would have a better chance to learn. There would be a meetinghouse for those who were not of Church of England loyalty. Town officers would be elected at regular times, courts held, taxes collected, and Representatives sent to the Massachusetts General Court. Best of all, because of this legal connection with another colony, Portsmouth and her neighbor towns now began to feel themselves part of a larger whole instead of four isolated settlements. As early as 1653 nowhere in New England were people thinking of themselves as Americans. They were members of Massachusetts colony, Connecticut colony, Rhode Island colony. Little by little they began to feel the need of union, most keenly for protection against the Indians. Later they discovered common interests and loyalties. All this takes time. It began to happen for Portsmouth with the annexation to Massachusetts.

From the new prosperity that came also with this union, she began also to develop the crafts and industries her port situation made natural for her—building ships, most of all. From the earliest days of Strawbery Banke she had made canoes, gundalows, shallops, small river craft, fishing boats, barges, and then gradually larger boats for coastwise shipping. For two hundred years and more, these would all be made of wood: mast, deck, keel, cabin. Even a boat's ornamentation would be of wood, skillfully fashioned. Ship carpenters were often artists in their use of wood for all that a ship required.

New Hampshire had many thousands of white pine, birch, and cedar, bordering her rivers for uncounted miles back into the wilderness. By the 1650s there were already an older and a younger generation who knew how to cut, trim, and transport wood for whatever need it might serve. The Mother Country had made woodsmen aware of the value of white pine, for from the earliest days the Crown had claimed "all white pines fit for masting our Royal Navy." All such trees should be preserved for that use alone. They belonged, said the royal Proclamation, "to His Majesty, his heirs and successors forever." Forever is a long time, but in the early years New Hampshire woodsmen did not complain loudly when the king's men cut their trees wherever they chose and took them in mast fleets to England. An ear of Indian corn presented to the captain of the "mast fleet" was a token of

A GUNDALOW *loaded with lumber. Scores of these boats carried heavy freight up and down the river. A yoke of oxen were often transported as passengers.*

good faith with the Mother Country. For a time they presented the ear of corn willingly.

Gradually, however, as the years went on, objections began to be heard. At first the Pine Acts of the Crown had demanded all white pine twenty-four inches in diameter two feet from the ground. As this demand was more and more ignored, the regulations tightened. All trees twelve inches across, three feet from the ground, were also claimed as belonging to the Crown. The word "oppression" began to be heard and woodsmen disobeyed more openly. The officers of the "mast fleet" became more severe in punishment for this disobedience, but it did not cease. Portsmouth was building smaller ships than the British navy in those years and she could use these smaller masts herself. The talk about "oppression" became louder.

The method of handling mast pine was the same whatever the length of the mast. Special treatment came at every stage of the process and trained skill was ready. It was skill with ax and saw, and skill in the handling of oxen especially— skill of hand always, engineering skill, but with little help of machinery. There were no chain saws in those days, no wires to plug in, no buttons to press, no levers to turn. Men and oxen did it all by their own trained strength and skill.

Finding a tree that would make a mast came first. It must be large at the base, straight to the very tip, and anywhere from fifty to seventy feet high. The standard ratio in measurement was three feet of length to every inch of diameter. For larger ships, the tree must be as tall as ninety to a hundred feet or more. When it was cut, it must fall in a lane that would fit its length and always with the base toward the river. This lane must be piled high with branches to make a cushion for the tree to fall on. This operation was called "bedding the tree." When it lay safely on its cushion of branches, another path must be cut from the base of the fallen tree to the river, sometimes a long way off. This path must be wide enough for as many pair of oxen to walk as the height of the tree required. Unless this path were straight, many more trees would have to be cut, for even a short mast could not be turned in the dense woods.

With the tree down and the path cut, it was time for the oxen to be brought. They were transported in gundalows down the river, or driven through the woods. Winter ice or snow made the pulling easier. At other seasons the mast was swung between giant wheels, five or six or even eight feet high. The oxen supplied the power. Samuel Sewall once spoke of seeing a mast hauled by thirty-two oxen in front and four at the sides. He called it "a very notable sight." Pulling, in any season, had its dangers, particularly if there were hills to cross. If a hill were steep, the yoke of oxen in the rear were lifted off the ground as the front end of the mast went over the top of the hill. Quick work by the man in front and great skill of the driver in the rear were needed to prevent disaster at this point. The rear oxen were sometimes killed, especially in moving the larger trees.

Guiding the mast into the river at the water's edge also took quick action and great skill. Lumbering has its perils in any age, and in spite of the long experience of New Hampshire woodsmen, things sometimes went wrong.

Once the great logs were in the water, the river took over, the men guiding the logs around bends, over rapids, through the narrows, and down perhaps many miles to Portsmouth and the ship carpenters. Even so, sometimes logs were lost or caught in a jam, sometimes broken, but the river was kind in saving strength of man and beast. A mast's safe arrival was always something of a triumph.

The mast trees of virgin pine along the Piscataqua disappeared generations ago, but hundreds of logs still float down New Hampshire rivers, not to shipyards but to sawmills and paper mills. More logs are now handled by one sawmill than by the seventy that were once New Hampshire's proud boast.

Shipbuilding in an age of sailing ships meant sailcloth, acres of it, and Portsmouth made it. Sailing vessels also needed rope and in amazing quantity. A full-rigged ship had many sails and every sail was edged with fine rope, called boltrope. There were bowlines attached to the side of the sail; a clewline at the lower corner of a square sail, a buntline from the middle part of a square sail, and leech lines to either edge. The mast was kept taut with ropes. The anchors were fastened to rope cables of great length and circumference. Small ships of course took less than square-riggers, but the sinews of every ship, large or small, were ropes.

Portsmouth did not buy her ropes. She made them. So did Boston, Portland, and every other seacoast town in New England. Rope was made in long, narrow buildings called rope walks. Ship rope can have no knots, so the rope walk had to be as long as the longest rope needed. By the end of the 1600s Boston had fourteen rope walks, one at the end of what is now the Public Garden. A century later there were a hundred and seventy-three rope walks in America and every one of them was needed. Such buildings no longer exist, now that machinery has taken over the patient hand-work of earlier times. The process is essentially the same, but manufacturing space is handled differently.

The poet Longfellow had been a boy in Portland, where there were still rope walks in the early nineteenth century, and he wrote verses about the one he knew. They bring back the picture. He remembered the steady hum of the wheel, not a loud sound, but "drowsy," as he says, a sound to go to sleep by.

> "In that building long and low,
> With its windows all a-row,
>   Like the portholes of a hulk,
> Human spiders spin and spin,
> Backwards down their threads so thin,
>   Dropping each, a hempen bulk.
>
> At the end, an open door,
> Squares of sunshine on the floor
>   Light the long and dusky lane;
> And the whirling of a wheel,
> Dull and drowsy makes me feel
>   All the spokes are in my brain.
>
> As the spinners to the end
> Downward go and reascend
>   Gleam the long threads in the sun;
> While within this brain of mine,
> Cobwebs brighter and more fine
>   By the busy wheel are spun."

He had seen the whole process and remembered the feeling the rope walk had given him, as well as the details before his eyes.

The ancient Chinese, Egyptians, Greeks, and Romans had made their rope in just the same way Longfellow describes. Machines today also use the same process, only far more quickly and easily. Unwind a piece of rope and the process almost becomes clear. There are three strands. Each strand is made up of many threads. Each of these threads is made up of many fibers. Today the fibers are made of nylon, or of manila from a species of the banana plant. In early America they were made of hemp, a plant of tough fiber, which grew plentifully in New England.

The process was a series of twists, three of them, and each twist in the opposite direction from the one immediately preceding. It sounds simple. The fibers are twisted toward the right to make the threads. The threads are twisted toward the left to form the strands. The strands are twisted toward the right to form the rope. The twists merely oppose each other. Anyone can prove this by experimenting for himself, although after the experiment he may agree that the process sounds simpler than it really is.

In those early days of the 1600s Portsmouth's rope walks were her chief factories and the building of ships her leading industry. But she also had many craftsmen employed in many sorts of skilled handwork. The making of furniture, the dyeing of cloth, the building of carriages employed many. There were also gunsmiths, tinsmiths, goldsmiths, silversmiths, clock and watch makers, jewellers. Her carpenters were among the best in New England. Some of the houses they built are some of the most beautiful still standing in New England, and they remain one of the city's distinctions. Nearly every street has its mansion. Hundreds of visitors come to see them every summer—the Wentworth House, the Warner House, the John Paul Jones House, and many others.

The earliest house still standing is the famous Jackson House, its roof sloping almost to the earth in the rear, its front on the river. Its frame is oak, one reason for its long preservation. In the lower rooms the sills project on the inner side, making seats for generations of children when chairs were scarcer than they are today. In 1663, from which this house dates, doubtless there were many houses in town built like this one, but today the Jackson House alone reminds us of home life as it was lived in these early years.

Families were large. The home was the center of life and also was almost completely independent so far as everything the family needed was concerned. The spacious kitchen was almost a factory of industry. The spinning wheel spun all the thread and yarn. The loom wove all the cloth. The mother wove all the blankets, sheets, and material for clothing. She made the clothes out of the material she had woven. She spun yarn and knitted stockings and caps. The father killed the animals whose fur was made into jackets, leggings, and the rug before the fire. Everything was done by hand and at home.

Food for the family was raised at home—the peas dried, the grain ground into meal at home until the first local grain

THE JACKSON HOUSE, *which was sturdily enough built to survive until the present day.*

mill was built. Every household made maple sugar for its own needs or kept bees for honey. Purchases at the general store were fewer than a modern family could easily imagine, and were usually made by exchanging some homegrown or homemade product. The result was almost complete independence under each home roof. Boys and girls learned the skills which helped to make this true.

School hours were few. Boys lived the outdoor life of their fathers and learned skill with gun, ax, and knife before they had gone far in learning to read and write. Girls learned the household crafts. Reading, writing, and "ciphering" or "figuring" were the subjects taught by the early schoolmaster. Geography, history, art, and what we call social studies were unknown in the schoolroom. Books of one's own were rare.

Every home was a farm, with acres to cultivate, domestic animals to care for, sheep to shear, cows to milk, hogs to butcher. Visits afar were rare. The sea at his door was every boy's world of adventure and his dream of far greater adventure. Someday he would sail away to the larger worlds beyond the river's mouth. Until then he learned to meet each day's surprise or danger as it came, for on the edge of endless woods no two days were ever quite the same. The adventure of his life might come before sunset.

~5~

Indians Come

UNTIL 1675 New Hampshire settlements had enjoyed more than a half century of peace with their nearest Indian neighbors, the Pennacooks. Sometimes there had been peace because the Indians feared the white man's gunpowder, sometimes the peace of real friendliness; but in 1675 all over New England it was tomahawks in angry Indian hands and a loaded musket for reply in English hands. Night by night garrison houses in every colony were filled with terrified inhabitants of every village and town.

Indian chiefs of all tribes had known for a long time that the white man would win, and some of them had counseled peace for their time. Passaconaway, the great sachem of the Pennacooks of the north, had been saying this to his people for a long time, although sometimes he too had been a warrior. When he was a hundred years old, and many of his tribe had assembled at a great feast to do him honor, he spoke his farewell in these words, as tradition reports:

"Hearken to the last words of your father and friend. The white men are sons of the morning. The Great Spirit is their Father. His sun shines brightly about them. Never make war upon them. Sure as you light the fires, the breath of heaven will turn the flames upon you, and destroy you. Listen to my advice. It is the last I shall ever give you. Remember it and live."

Tradition also says that after speaking these words Passaconaway disappeared in cloud and thunder.

His people believed what he had said for a time. He had been a man of great power and in their thoughts also a magician. They liked to tell that he could make water burn, trees dance, and green leaves grow out of ashes. Once, they said he had made a live snake arise from the skin of a dead one.

But these magic tales were forgotten when what the history books call King Philip's War became every Indian's war. They remembered only their own grievances against the English. They were being pushed off their lands. The white man's sawmills had spoiled the rivers for fishing and the woods for hunting. He had put fences around the lands Indians had sold to him. Why? He tried Indians by white man's laws and always found them guilty. Why? Passaconaway's son, Wonalancet, was a gentler man than his father and not a strong leader in troubled times. They did not listen to him as they had to his father, the magic sachem.

King Philip's Indian name was Metacomet. He was a Wampanoag, the son of Massasoit, another of the great sachems of New England's first generation. When Massasoit died, Philip took over and was called King instead of Sachem. He had many grievances against the English. When his brother died mysteriously, he suspected the English of poisoning him. When his tribe was steadily pushed farther backward, he was resentful, and when three of his tribesmen were executed because of their supposed murder of a Christian messenger and all of its members ordered to surrender their arms, he would bear no more. He marshaled his own tribe, the Wampanoags, won the Nipmucks and the Narragansetts to fight with him against the whites, and then inflamed them all to wage the most destructive Indian war in New England history. Scores of English men, women, and children were savagely murdered, their towns were burned, their sheep and cattle destroyed. For a time it looked as though English settlements in New England were all doomed, and that all the whites would be killed. In the first year of the war, the Indians won everywhere.

The Pennacooks in the north did not stage a big war against their neighboring Piscataqua settlements. Instead, they attacked scattered settlements, coming in parties of only eight or ten, killing the men of the family, and carrying off the women and children. They burned houses and barns behind them and slaughtered the cattle. The larger towns escaped for the most part, Portsmouth among them.

Oyster River in the Dover region was their first target. With a small party of attacking Indians they killed two men, carried off two captives, and burned two houses. Two days later they attacked Richard Tozer's house at Salmon Falls where fifteen women and children had taken refuge. A young girl succeeded in holding the door until the women and children had escaped out the back way and run through the bushes to a better fortified house nearby. The Indians broke down the door with hatchets, struck the girl, and left her for dead. She recovered, however, and lived many years. Two small children who had not succeeded in getting over the fence were carried off. This was a typical raid in this section, and there were many of them. The whole countryside was terrified. Safety lay only in the larger settlements, and not always there. Sudden attacks in the isolated neighborhoods went on for months.

Over and over it was the same story. A door left open while a man went to milk the cow or bring in wood. An Indian watching his chance behind a tree. A war whoop at night and the family awakened to find their barn in flames and Indians at their door. Always in a different place and always without warning. No one was safe. Bushes along any path might conceal Indians. In the north they were not in an army. They were in small groups skulking, just a few, tomahawks in hand.

In 1676 King Philip was killed—not by an Englishman, but by a traitor Indian. Separated from his men, he was led into a swamp on Mt. Hope by one traitor and shot by another as he ran down the only path of escape. With his death, the great war was over. With their leader gone, the Wampanoags and their allies were helpless. Given time to organize their defense, the Englishmen of Massachusetts were all soldiers now, and they had adopted the Indian ways of fighting. No Indian in Massachusetts was safe. Troops of soldiers were everywhere hunting them down. There was no place to hide.

Scores of King Philip's surviving men fled northward and tried to mingle with the Pennacooks. They were hungry, and also afraid the Massachusetts soldiers would still catch up with them, for they were close behind. Cold weather had come, and the Indians had no blankets. Wonalancet would not deal with them. They were unwelcome to his people. Some of the skulkers who were attacking New Hampshire neighborhoods were members of this desperate band.

In September of the year 1676, a large number of these desperate men, some two hundred, we are told, went to Major Waldron in Dover to ask for food and protection. They had heard that only the year before he had made peace with the Pennacooks when they returned the captives they had taken; perhaps he would be kinder than Wonalancet. Major Waldron was a great man in his neighborhood in his day. Possibly no one in the whole region had done more for Dover in his generation. He was one of its early settlers, a builder of mills, a trader in lumber, and had been five times elected Speaker of the House. He had dealt with Indians all his life and had had a chance to learn much about their ways. But this time he forgot some things he should have remembered.

The time itself was most unfortunate, for on the same day the fugitive Indians came for help a large number of Pennacooks also arrived, surrounding Major Waldron's house and asking to have conference with him. The reason for their coming is not known, but very likely it concerned the presence in the neighborhood of two companies of Massachusetts soldiers in pursuit of Philip's fugitives. The presence of all these Indians in their town, more than half of their own whole population, terrorized the English settlement. No wonder. It was a situation that called for a cool head, great wisdom, and tact.

Naturally the Massachusetts soldiers wanted to seize the southern Indians at once, and send them back to Boston for imprisonment or sale into slavery.

"No," said Major Waldron. "We shall not do that. We shall try a stratagem." That was his mistake.

No one knew what he had in mind. The Pennacooks, remembering the recent peace he had made with them, thought he was still their friend and obeyed his orders. The southern Indians apparently suspected no harm. They thought they were being rescued from the Massachusetts soldiers and they obeyed also. As the story is reported, the Major announced that they would all have a *training* together, Indians and whites. Accordingly, he lined them all up, Indians in front and whites behind. They obeyed. He then ordered the Indians to fire first. They did so. Immediately every Indian was seized, Pennacook and southern Indians alike, disarmed, and held fast. Not a man was hurt on either side. Wonalancet, chief of the Pennacooks, was told that his men would all be freed, as they were. But the fugitive Indians were bound by the soldiers, imprisoned, and later put on a ship for Boston. Several who were known to be murderers were executed, and all the others sold into slavery in the West Indies.

Some protests were made, but the fugitive Indians were gone from the Piscataqua country, and Major Waldron took pride in the neatness of his "stratagem." He had solved the present problem, he thought. But he had forgotten all he knew about Indians. The Pennacooks would never forget his deceit, nor would they ever trust him again. More than that, they would have their revenge. For an Indian to deceive a white man was one thing, but for a white man to deceive an Indian, as the Indians thought, was quite another. Major Waldron should have known this.

Thirteen years later, when Major Waldron was an old man, and all had been peaceable for a long time between Indians and whites, more Indians than usual began to come into the Dover region. They seemed peaceful, but why so many of them? The residents grew worried. Day after day more Indians came. More of the people became alarmed, but not Major Waldron. When friends, both Indian and white, came to warn him, he laughed and said, "Go, and plant your pumpkins."

One morning an Indian squaw came, singing,

> "O Major Waldron, you great sagamore,
> What will you do, Indians at your door?"

Still the Major was not alarmed.

A messenger sent from Governor Bradstreet in Boston to warn him was detained at the ferry (possibly by Indian plan) and arrived one day too late, June 28. For on June 27, just at dusk, two Indian squaws came to the door of the garrison house where Major Waldron slept, and asked for the favor of sleeping there that night. In peaceful times, this was a favor often granted, but one wonders why no one was suspicious that night. Permission was given, and the squaws were shown how to open the door if they came late or wanted to leave early in the morning. No one took the trouble to inquire of the other garrison houses, but later it appeared that two squaws had come to each of them at dusk with the same request. Early that evening a friendly Indian had asked the Major:

"Brother Waldron, what would you do if the strange Indians should come?"

"I would assemble a hundred men," he answered, "by lifting up my finger."

No watch was set, and the various households went to bed as usual. At midnight the two squaws opened the doors of each of the garrison houses and the waiting strange Indians rushed in. They did not know in which of the houses the Major was sleeping. But it was too late now. Their torch-light in his face, his room full of Indians, and a savage war whoop in his ears awakened him for the last time. He grasped the sword which lay by his side, but his murderers were too quick for him. He was overpowered, struck down, bound with rope, and laid on the table.

"Who shall judge Indians now?" they mocked as they marched around the table, each Indian giving him a gash with a knife as they passed. The families sleeping in the garrison houses were also killed and their homes burned. Revenge had been long in coming, but here it was and not for Major Waldron alone.

The score against the Major satisfied, the Indian uprising was soon put down. The strange Indians went home and all was quiet around Dover, but it had been a sad return of earlier terrors, and like every other raid, aroused new fears for months to come. Until the end of the century, there were other uprisings occasionally, once at Portsmouth.

Boys and girls of the Piscataqua towns for the space of several generations had been taken to garrison houses night after night almost since they had been born. There was hardly a boy or girl in the whole region who had not been awakened by war whoops, gunshots more than once, or perhaps had seen his own home in flames. In many a home some child was missing, carried off in an Indian raid. Often, in fact usually, the captured children were treated kindly, for if kept healthy, they could be sold to the French for a good price, and Indians always wanted money. Sometimes if the children had been carried off too young to remember their own homes, they grew up with the Indian children, sometimes married within the tribe, and stayed for life. More often they were found and redeemed shortly after they were taken.

John Stark, the famous New Hampshire general of Revolutionary days, had been carried off as a young boy and kept for only three months before he was found. He was redeemed for an Indian pony worth $120. He always said that he had a good time with the Indians and learned many things valuable to him. He liked best to tell of having been set to the task of hoeing the Indian corn. Instead of cutting the weeds, he hoed up the corn and saved the weeds. When the Indians discovered what he had done, they demanded to know why. "Hoeing corn is for squaws," he answered, "not for warriors." The Indians liked his answer and called him "Young Chief." They were sorry to lose him when he was redeemed by his people. He also liked to tell that when he was first captured, he was forced to run between two lines of warriors armed with clubs. This was an Indian custom with captives. John Stark seized the club of the first Indian in the line, and used it on him with such force that the whole line scurried out of aim. The old warriors who were watching this test were amused, and laughed at their own young men. They liked "Young Chief."

Other boys were not always redeemed so quickly. There is the tale of Jonathan Dorr, who was sitting on the fence of his own home lot, singing a song, when he was suddenly captured; and he was not found for twelve years, although he had been kindly treated. There is the tale of the young girl who, after being made to walk twelve miles before her Indian captors, was given the flesh of a dog to eat. She refused to touch it. A friendly Indian, knowing she was hungry, took his gun, killed a woodpecker, and prepared it for her supper. When she was found by her family, the ransom demanded was her weight in silver, which was a larger sum than her family could pay. A white doctor in the rescuing party told the Indians that she was sick, would not live long, and was not worth such a large sum. Let her go for less, he pleaded, and she was finally redeemed for $18.50. A pleasant end to her story is that she lived to be a hundred years old.

Before Indian raids were finally over, there had been more than a half century of warfare to match the half century of peace that had preceded. Indians had not always been enemies of the English during this time, but they had become allies of the French in the long-continued French and Indian wars against the British for the possession of Canada. The wars of the two mother countries became the wars of the French and English colonies who might otherwise have lived peaceably with the Indians of America through many years of that warlike half century.

If the Indians had written the story of those wars and of the scores of border raids which cost so many lives, destroyed so much property, and caused so much bitterness and cruelty, our sympathy with the Indians might have been much greater than many of the history books have allowed it to be. The Indians lost their lands, their freedom to roam the wilderness, and also many thousands of their people. They did not understand the white man's ways, and too often the white man did not try to understand their ways. He learned Indian cruelties and practiced them. Indians scalped whites and whites scalped Indians. Indians burned the homes of whites and whites burned Indian villages, sparing neither women or children. The story of Indians and whites has many sad chapters and there was much wrong on both sides.

~6~

Robert Rogers Leads
the Rangers

THE GREAT Indian war was over, but other wars came. Every war brought new dangers and changed many things; it also created new heroes. For the boys and girls of the mid-eighteenth century in Portsmouth one of the new and longest remembered heroes was Robert Rogers, world-famous leader of the world-famous Rangers.

Robert Rogers was not a native of Portsmouth, but was born at Methuen, Massachusetts, on the very edge of the wilderness. The woods was his childhood world. His father, James Rogers, was a squatter, struggling to support his family on the few acres he had cleared. When Robert was seven, his family together with a neighboring family moved to New Hampshire, where both fathers had secured small tracts of land in the area known as Great Meadow. Here Robert's father built a house and planted fruit trees. He plowed fields that had grown grass for centuries, but had never before been touched by a plow. The several small boys in these two families began to grow up in this lonely spot ten miles from the nearest town.

The woods and its creatures were their teachers. There was no schoolhouse. Occasionally a friendly Indian taught them secrets no schoolmaster might have known: how to walk and leave no tracks, how to find a trail with their feet in the night, how to keep their direction through the dense woods by sun, moon, and stars. They learned birdcalls and could imitate them so that even the birds were deceived. They learned animal haunts and ways, and knew what to do at the first signal of danger. They could read Indian ax marks on tree trunks as a language. With all this knowledge came a rare courage. In a life made of danger they learned safety. Perhaps best of all, they learned it early. After only seven years in Great Meadow, when Robert was just fourteen, war struck the frontier. This changed his life.

Small parties of French and Indians were making raids on isolated farms in the neighborhood. At first the two families stayed on their small homesteads keeping watch. Then one night a horseman in swift alarm rode down the narrow bridle path at dusk and warned them to flee. They groped their way ten miles through the night to Rumford. In the morning when they went back home, they found their houses in smoking ruins, their cattle slaughtered, and the tiny fruit trees cut down—all but one lone apple tree.

Young Robert was a boy under the family roof no longer. He became a surveyor of roads, a climber of the White Mountains, an explorer of rivers, as one assignment in his training followed another. This practical use of his earlier experiences made him afraid of nothing in nature. The tougher the problem, the better he liked to risk finding a solution.

When he was twenty-four years old, a call went out for volunteers in the Canadian campaign. They were to embark for Nova Scotia and drive the French from the Bay of Fundy. Robert not only volunteered himself, but when he reached the encampment, he had brought with him fifty other New Hampshire men besides. These men became "Company I" to answer the call. Crown Point was their goal, but it took a long time to get there. When they were as far north as Albany, Robert was selected for the convoying of provisions up the Hudson to the camp called Great Carrying Place. Meanwhile the French had attacked at Lake George and escaped. No one had pursued them. Where were they hiding? How many men were in the company? What would they do next? General William Johnson needed to know, and promptly. Miles of dense forest must be passed through to find out. There were no guides experienced in this region. It was just the assignment for Robert Rogers. His life since childhood had prepared him for this sort of perilous journey. He was chosen to go, make observations, and report back. Time was precious. He must go at once.

On a dark September night a small flat-bottomed boat slipped into the lake. With four other men he rowed all night. At dawn they pulled the boat out of the water at a leafy inlet and hid it under the trees. Two of the men were left to guard it. Robert and the other two stepped into the dark woods and in less than half a minute had gone into the utter silence. It took two days and twelve hours to get through the woods to a point where the French fort of St. Frederick was in full view beyond the trees. There had been no trail. No enemy scouts had followed. Robert and his men had made no fires. Cold dried beef had been their food. September nights were chill, and there were thousands of mosquitoes. To those who were called Rangers all this was unimportant.

From their hidden point of observation in the trees, they noted the fort, the barracks, the drawbridge, the tents. They estimated the number of troops, the equipment, the apparent sense of safety—for no watch was set for the night. When all was quiet, the troops asleep, Robert and his two companions started on the long way back, only to find when they reached the place where the boat had been hidden, that the two men left to guard it had gone. Tired of waiting, they had rowed back to the Lake George camp. This meant that three tired, hungry men must walk the entire distance, threading their way through unfamiliar woods. They arrived safely, having been absent nine days, and brought the report they had been sent to get.

This success was only the beginning. Six days later Rogers slipped out again with four other men to investigate the French stronghold at Ticonderoga. On this trip by canoe, he sighted an encampment of several thousand French and Indians, was pursued, escaped, and returned safely to camp with his report. Two Indian scouts contradicted him and an intended offensive was not carried out. Winter was coming on; many soldiers wanted to go home, and did so, even General Johnson himself. Robert Rogers and a small remnant were left in the half-finished fort at Lake George.

What took place during those lonely winter months brought Robert Rogers his first fame. He continued the scouting, sometimes on skates, sometimes on snowshoes. Bitter weather was to him no reason for lying idle. He believed in offensive warfare, something new in wintertime fighting in his day and therefore not expected by the enemy. With small parties of fifty or sixty men he made raids on the outskirts of the French camp, first at one point and then at another. He set fires, and destroyed enemy supplies, always at some new point, distant from the last raid. His men were never seen, coming or going. They moved in silence. Their signals were birdcalls. No shot was ever permitted in their journey. Whenever they slept, half of the company watched. When they moved, someone was always looking behind for a possible follower.

News of these raids reached Boston, at the headquarters of General Shirley, chief of the British forces in America. Shirley summoned Rogers for questioning. The outcome of this meeting was more Rangers, and immediately. They were to do what Rogers and his men had been doing all winter; keep the French in constant alarm, capture their messengers, find out the French positions and their strength, and discover routes over which the New England army might reach them. Rangers must be experienced in hunting and tracking, be hardy enough for long marches and severe exposure. They would be supplied with warm clothing and well paid. Robert Rogers was to recruit them at once.

By April he and his brother had signed up a troop of New Hampshire men, and they were immediately off to the north, half of the company under each of the brothers. Many Portsmouth men were in this company. John Stark was one of the lieutenants. They went to work first in one place and then in another. They seemed to be everywhere. In terms of figures, what they did might seem small. Not many men were killed, not many prisoners taken, but both friend and foe knew of Robert Rogers. His name began to be heard in France and England. His exploits had also put heart into hundreds of New England soldiers.

Cutting the French line of communication between Canada and Crown Point by capturing the messengers and keeping them as prisoners was one of his most brilliant performances. He did this with fifty men in whaleboats, ten men to a boat. They rowed down the lake by night in utter quietness, pulled their boats out of the water, and hid them while they watched all day. Later they carried the boats on their backs a distance of four miles from Lake George to Wood Creek. Before this exploit was over, he had penetrated into the very center of enemy territory, taken the messengers as prisoners, and returned to camp with all his men safe. The effect on the American troops was electric. His successes were the only ones in the campaign of 1756. More Rangers, said the High Command.

More Rangers enlisted and were carefully trained. Asked

MAJOR ROBERT ROGERS *of the Rangers. This supposed likeness of Robert Rogers was sold in London in 1776 as one of a series of "rebel officers." There is doubt as to its truth to his features. The two Indian-decorated belts slung over his left shoulder, the high "Indian stockings," and the Indians in the background may be part of the deception.*

to set down his method of training, Robert Rogers noted these items:

"Training is always in the evening.

Each man's equipment is carefully examined. He should have a firelock, a tomahawk, a scalping knife, a bullock's horn full of powder, a sealskin bag of bullets and smaller shot, and a small compass in the bottom of the bag.

Every man must be ready to march at a moment's notice.

Before dismissal the next day's plans are named and a place of meeting given in case we are separated. This place is always different from the one named the day before.

There are eight or ten men in each patrol.

We walk single file, and far enough apart so that one enemy shot cannot hit two men at the same time.

On mossy ground we change positions and walk abreast so that the enemy cannot track us.

Signals are birdcalls, and we make a language of them.

If surrounded, we wait for darkness and each goes to the place of meeting by a different route.

During the night, half of the party watch. There is no noise during the change of watch.

We never halt except on high ground.

Our battle lines are two deep.

We keep a sharp watch just at daylight. This is the Indian's striking hour.

At meal time we keep a sharp watch behind us, on the path we came in.

We always avoid the usual fords and paths."

These rules sound easy enough and simple enough, but they could hardly be safely followed by men who did not know the New England woods and weathers and how to be at home in them. Backwoods warfare is for men born to the wilderness.

Robert Rogers seemed to have ingenuity for dealing with whatever new danger presented itself. Once when surrounded on three sides by pursuing Indians, on the shore of Lake George, he made his way on snowshoes to the top of a high rock overhanging the lake. This was the only free direction he could take. Once at the top, he threw his haversack and equipment over the cliff. He then put on his snowshoes backward and fastened them very tightly. Walking very carefully, he went down, making another path close to the one he had used when coming up.

The Indians found the tracks and followed them to the top: two tracks up; no track down. Where was he? Then they saw him far away escaping on the ice. The Great Spirit had protected him, they thought, and taken him over the precipice on wings. "Rogers' Slide," this spot was called afterward. It is still pointed out.

Throughout the seven years of war, the victories of the Rangers were won time after time by the same strategy Robert Rogers used in his own personal escapes. Surprise was the keynote. Never do what they expect. Don't wait for them to come. Go after them. Be completely secret. It worked, at least nearly always. Nothing mattered but to have victory. When supplies were gone, he and his men ate mushrooms, dug lily bulbs, ground nuts, and even chewed the leather on their cartridge belts, if they were not lucky enough to find a squirrel.

During these same years Portsmouth came to know Robert Rogers as one of their own, and not only as a hero. They knew him as a person. As he went back and forth from various Canadian points to Boston, he made brief stops there. He spent his leave there more than once. Young and old took him to their hearts. Portsmouth boys and men had served with him as Rangers. On one occasion of leave, he was invited to join a local lodge of which the Reverend Arthur Browne, rector of St. John's chapel, was the chaplain. Whether his interest in Mr. Browne's fourteen-year-old daughter dates from this occasion or another we do not know, but six years later Elizabeth Browne, the belle of the town, became the bride of Robert Rogers. This marriage, of course, made him more than ever a very special person in Portsmouth.

History is people as well as wars and treaties of peace, and a town that can claim a famous hero either of peace or war is fortunate indeed. Robert Rogers was a soldier from his fourteenth year and his deeds were an inspiration to thousands of his countrymen in a dangerous time. No wonder that Portsmouth treasures his memory, and in very special ways. They count him one of their own.

⁓ 7 ⁓

The Sons of Liberty March

VERY SOON the men who had won French Canada for England shouldered arms again to win New England for themselves and to be free from the Mother Country. There were only fifteen years between the French and Indian war and the American Revolution, and these were not peaceful years. The generation of New England boys who grew up during these troubled years knew that they would soon be soldiers. They took sides for or against England as their fathers and uncles and older brothers were doing. Nearly every household during these years had at least one Tory, as those who were loyal to England were called. Arguments at home and in the neighborhood were often bitter. Wars fought on the school playground were no longer Indian wars, but boys' wars between England and her American colonies.

The French and Indian war had been a war of conquest. Both sides had wanted land and the power that comes with the possession of land. The Revolution was a war of loyalties. To the Tory it was loyalty to the Mother Country. To the colonist it was loyalty to his own country. He would make her free. Both are ideals for which men have fought and died in all ages of the world.

During those fifteen years of peace before open war broke out, Portsmouth had been prosperous. Hundreds of new settlers had come to each of the four towns on the Piscataqua and the wide spaces between, now free from Indian raids. Roads that had been cut through the woods for marching armies and their supply wagons during the French and Indian war were now traffic lanes connecting new settlements with the larger towns. The first regular stage-coach in America had begun to run from Portsmouth to Boston once a week. It could carry three passengers, was drawn by two horses, and the fare was three dollars. This new connection with the largest town in New England opened a very important door to Portsmouth, and her people used it freely.

New problems, of course, came with this new convenience, but the town meeting knew how to solve them. When small-pox in Boston was carried to Portsmouth by stagecoach and boat, a fence was ordered built across the road at Great Swamp and a small house set up at that point. In this house passengers and their baggage were "smoked" for a time thought to make them safe from infection. All boat passengers from Boston were similarly treated before they were allowed to land. Vaccination would come very soon to this section of New England, as it had already come farther south, but in the early 1760s "smoking" was the plan of the Portsmouth selectmen.

Along the river and far back into the woods many new sawmills had been built and water power harnessed. Many gundalows, heavily loaded with logs, went down the river to Portsmouth docks. Much lumber was being sold abroad. Merchants were prospering. More houses were being built. It seemed that a time of great promise had come.

But along with this new prosperity came troubling old problems and more troubling new ones. Among the old ones was England's claim to more and more tall pines for her own ships. The King's broad ax mark seemed to be everywhere and the "Mast Men" more insistent. New Hampshire woodsmen became more disobedient, and many a tree marked with the broad arrow was cut and put on their own gundalows for export. Owners began to talk of their rights, and to pronounce the word as though it were written in capitals.

When John Mason's heir, Robert Mason, renewed his demands for rent from the land New Hampshire men had cleared nearly a century and a half before, their grandsons pronounced the word RIGHTS in capitals again. The land was theirs and Robert Mason would not have a cent of rental. A new spirit was in the land, and the generosity of John Mason, their founder, was fast becoming a dim memory.

But the Stamp Act was the major issue in the mid-1760s and all New England was in open and vigorous rebellion.

The colonies were being taxed by the Mother Country without their consent. They would not submit to such a law or allow it to stand on the books. Excitement flamed in every town and village. Violence was only a step away.

This Act touched nearly everyone's life at some point. The hated stamp, printed in England, must be attached to every deed for land, bill of lading, marriage license, will, diploma, bond, and newspaper advertisement, and the tax paid before the transaction was completed. Worse still, offenders would have no trial by their own fellows. A court of admiralty (British) would decide all cases. It was oppression, the colonists said, and they said it with anger. A sales tax today arouses the residents of any state, but they do not take up their guns and load them. Their own representatives have voted the tax, but that had not happened in 1765. The Stamp Act was imposed by the Mother Country without the consent of the colonies, and they would not endure it.

The immediate opposition of the colonists surprised the royal governors and may have surprised the citizens who voiced it, as in one town after another they staged a demonstration. Usually this meant setting up a Liberty Pole. Nearly every town had one. Nearly every town also had a band of Liberty Boys, or Sons of Liberty, who usually set up the pole and led the demonstrations around it. No one knows just how these Sons of Liberty were first organized, but very probably the first recruits came from those in every town who had sharp grievances against the Mother Country. When the announcement of the Stamp Act first reached the colonies, these groups found each other, and all at once the Liberty Boys were everywhere, with new recruits every day. They became a force in town after town, and as the name gained dignity, they had much to do with stirring up patriotic feelings and making rebellion against oppression effective. With such groups growing more and more active in every settlement, and always a more conservative group opposing them, violence would soon follow, and then would come war.

Opposition to the Stamp Act in Portsmouth came promptly. The law was to go into effect on November 1, 1765. George Meserve, a native of the town, was to be the agent to distribute the stamps in New Hampshire. No citizen of Portsmouth ever had a more unpopular mission. Fortunately he was in England at the time news of his appointment reached his fellow townsmen, or he would have been roughly handled. When he reached Boston and learned the situation, he immediately resigned the appointment. Even so, Portsmouth was prepared to show him how they felt. On the morning he was expected to arrive, a dummy figure of him, along with one of Lord Bute, head of the British ministry, and one of the devil, were publicly exhibited at the Parade, an open space at the very center of the town.

All day Portsmouth dishonored these three figures, jeered at them and abused them. At night the three effigies were carried through the streets in a torchlight procession and then publicly burned. Everyone came, paraded, and spoke their minds. A week later, when George Meserve dared to come home, he was surrounded, jeered at, and had much difficulty convincing his fellow townsmen that he had resigned his commission and would not distribute the hated stamps. Finally, at the demand of the people, he went to the Parade and made a public statement of his resignation. They were forced to believe him. But the Stamp Act still stood on the books and November 1 was very near.

On the day before the Act was to go into effect, October 31, *The New Hampshire Gazette,* published in Portsmouth, appeared with heavy black borders, as a sign that Liberty was dead in New Hampshire. The editor stated that the paper would no longer be published, as the printer would not submit to the tax. Every advertisement had to have a stamp, and neither would the merchants advertise any longer. The *Gazette* was dead.

That same morning hundreds of men and women from the villages and scattered settlements around began to arrive. They marched up and down the streets, making it very clear that they had come to prevent any stamps from being distributed on that day. Bells tolled. All flags were at half-mast, in the town and on all the vessels in the harbor. The mood was ominous.

At three o'clock a funeral procession formed at the State House in the Parade. Out of the door on King Street came the Liberty Boys bearing a coffin which bore the inscription "LIBERTY, aged 145 years." This, of course, meant 1620, the year that the Pilgrims had landed on Plymouth Rock. Minute guns were fired, bells tolled, drums were muffled, as the procession moved slowly down the street, everyone following. When it reached the grave that had been dug, a speech was solemnly delivered, stating that Liberty, alive since 1620, was now dead.

But just as the coffin was being lowered, someone shouted that there were signs of life in the coffin. A troop of Sons of Liberty rushed forward, rescued the figure of a woman representing Liberty from the coffin, and carried her off in triumph. Quickly someone put the Proclamation of the Stamp Act in her place. The coffin was lowered and the grave quickly filled. Everyone within range threw a clod, and when the hole was heaped high, the Liberty Boys stamped on the top, making all the noise they could. Bells rang, joyously now, cannons were fired, the flags went up, and everyone shouted. At night a huge bonfire was lighted on Windmill Hill and everyone contributed his own noise of jubilation. Swing Bridge, near where the Liberty Pole stood, was immediately named Liberty Bridge.

When such demonstrations were repeated in town after town, Parliament was astonished at the fierceness of the resentment and the fervor of colonial patriotism the Stamp Act had aroused. Argument was long, but repeal came in the following year, 1766. When the news reached New England, celebrations of jubilation were held everywhere, but they had a grim note in them as well as rejoicing. All the colonies were now alert to other hints of *oppression,* one of the words of the hour. In Portsmouth both jubilation and the note of warning sounded promptly after news of repeal came. Bells began to ring at dawn and rang all day. A battery of guns dedicated to His Majesty, George III, was erected at Liberty Bridge, another dedicated to William Pitt at Church Hill, and a third at the town wharf. Ships in the harbor were decorated. At noon a royal salute was fired and answered by the town. At night there was another bonfire on Windmill Hill, with a bomb in the top of it—the more noise the better. When the bomb exploded, a great shout went up.

Repeal of the Stamp Act, however, did not end the sense of grievance.

Portsmouth's protests corresponded to those of Boston for the imposition of duties. One incident followed another. Once citizens in disguise carrying large clubs tied up the crew of a ship unloading molasses, one of the cargoes carrying a duty. In 1773, six days after the Boston Tea Party, Portsmouth held a private meeting, made a resolution, and each time tea arrived, they paid the duty, but shipped the tea to Halifax, which was British territory. No one in Portsmouth would drink it. Had they dumped the tea into the sea instead, history might have given them a page instead of a single sentence.

Similarly, history books say nothing about the ride of Paul Revere to Portsmouth on December 13, 1774. If there had been bloodshed that night this might have been the date of the beginning of the Revolution instead of April 19, 1775. But Portsmouth remembers that ride and that night.

Fort William and Mary in Portsmouth harbor was full of gunpowder and the British were sending two regiments of soldiers to guard it. Word that they were on the way

FORT WILLIAM AND MARY, *once a stronghold of defense at the very gate of the town.*

came to the Boston Committee of Safety and there was not a moment to lose. Portsmouth must get the powder before the soldiers arrived. Who would warn them? Paul Revere, of course. He had already carried messages of warning and had not been suspected. He knew how to get a pass out of the Boston gates, and he did it again this time. He approached slowly and then ambled at a leisurely pace until he was well out of sight. Then the ride became a race.

Snow on the ground, sixty miles to go, and speed all-important, but Paul Revere could set a record. All night in the cold moonlight and until afternoon of the next day he rode, drawing up at John Sullivan's house on the Oyster River, a short distance from Portsmouth.

While Paul Revere cared for his horse and caught a few winks of sleep, John Sullivan sped the news to the local Sons of Liberty, that the soldiers were coming, and with John Langdon as his co-worker plans were completed before dusk. No one went to sleep in Portsmouth that night. Four hundred Sons of Liberty assembled on the dock. Others brought the gundalows. Everyone was ready. Governor

PORTSMOUTH

Wentworth heard what was afoot and sent word to Captain Corcoran at the Fort that an assault was coming. The Captain had only four men with him, but he wheeled his four-pounders into position, and as he said later in his report to Governor Wentworth, "I did everything in my power to defend the Fort." But he was helpless.

Down the river in the moonlight came the gundalows. The Sons of Liberty went aboard. Then quietly, with not a word of conversation, just the soft plashing of the oars, the first boats drew up at the ledge some three hundred feet from the wall of the Fort. The Sons of Liberty demanded surrender. *Certainly not,* and instantly the four-pounders were fired, the gunners being careful the balls went well above the heads of the men in the gundalows. War was ahead, that was clear, but let the New Englanders spill the first blood. More gundalows drew toward the landing and the second demand for surrender was more insistent than the first. Surrender came. There was no other answer to make. The harbor was full of gundalows.

Captain Corcoran and his four men were bound but not hurt. The New Hampshire men then pulled down the king's flag and went to work on the powder. For an hour and a half these Sons of Liberty, stripped to the waist, waded back and forth in the icy water, carrying keg after keg of powder to the boats. They took ninety-nine kegs and left one. They also took all the small arms. Icy water on a December night was a test of endurance, even for men who knew the hardships of the frontier, but these men met it, and every one of the ninety-nine kegs was safely stowed in the gundalows. Captain Corcoran and his four men were untied, and the invaders were gone. They had not fired a shot.

The night was long enough for the gundalows to make the return trip up the river still in the moonlight. They were met by ox teams which carried the precious powder to safe hiding places, not known to this day. Loyal patriots, however, knew where every pound of it was hidden until, within a fortnight, it was taken to Bunker Hill and used. Paul Revere saddled his horse and carried the word of this night's work back to Boston. General Gage, British commander in chief, was enraged. The Minute Men rejoiced. The British officers stationed in Boston had been confident that farmer-soldiers would not dare what had not only been dared but successfully accomplished that winter night in Portsmouth harbor. The king's fort had been rifled. The flag of England had been taken down. Governor Wentworth issued an order that the powder be immediately returned and that loyal English subjects in Portsmouth volunteer at once as guards in the fort. Not a man in Portsmouth answered the call, and, of course, the powder remained where it was hidden. The first organized action of revolt against the Mother Country had taken place. Shots had been fired but as yet they were not heard around the world.

Meanwhile everyone listened in every town of every colony—swift horses' hooves in the night, when would they come, summoning the men and boys who were waiting to go? Once again it was the hoofbeats of Paul Revere's horse. Within minutes, drums beat, men in their farm clothes were marching, guns and ammunition ready. In one town after another they met on the Common, in the meetinghouse, long enough only to choose a leader, and they were off. Fifty-four men from Rindge, New Hampshire, were in Cambridge, Massachusetts, in two days. Ninety men from Keene, New Hampshire, marched eighty-five miles in two days. Two hundred men from Nottingham were twenty-seven miles on their way by dusk, and they were parading in Cambridge in twenty hours, with fifty-five miles behind them.

John Stark, who had been Robert Rogers' lieutenant in his Rangers, left his sawmill and was in Boston with two thousand men four days after the Lexington fight. Some of the Rangers were with him, men whose endurance sounds like a fable, yet they boasted only of their marksmanship. John Stark's standard was to hit a target the size of a dollar at the distance of a hundred yards. When the ammunition of the Americans gave out at Bunker Hill, it was John Stark who protected their retreat behind the rail fence, which his foresight had made a famous detail of the fight.

John Stark, Israel Putnam, and William Prescott are each credited with each of the oft-quoted words to the soldiers:

"Wait till you see the whites of their eyes!"
"Pick out the officers. Aim low."
"Fire at the crossing of the belts."

Whichever man spoke which word, that is what the soldiers did, and their careful aim made this engagement a

GENERAL JOHN STARK.
*A portrait painted late
in life. At the time of
the Bunker Hill battle,
he was only forty-eight
years old. He died in
1822 at ninety-four.*

costly victory for the British. Stark's men were in retreat, for their ammunition was exhausted, but thanks to the rail fence he lost only fifteen men and had forty-five wounded; the British lost more than a thousand.

One version of Stark's part in this battle, which may be tradition, shows him stepping to the front of his company, placing a stick in the ground, and announcing,

"There, don't a man fire till the redcoats come up to that stick. If he does, I'll knock him down."

At least the words fit Stark's explosive way of demanding obedience and imparting spirit in a desperate moment.

His greatest fame as leader of the New Hampshire troops

came in the battle of Bennington toward the end of the war. After sulking at home for a long period because he had not been promoted as he thought he deserved, after Bunker Hill, he resigned his command. This was in March, 1777, a crucial time for the Continental army. Victory seemed far off. General Burgoyne, in supreme command of the British northern army, was on his way to join the army of Sir William Howe at Albany and do battle with General Washington. If he succeeded in bringing the two British forces together, their chances looked bright. It was a dark moment for the Americans.

This was the time when John Langdon, who three years before had been the co-leader with John Sullivan in taking the powder from Fort William and Mary, stood up in the Exeter Assembly and made the speech that Portsmouth still remembers.

"Gentlemen," he said, " I have $5000 in hard money; my plate I will pledge for as much more. I have seventy hogsheads of Tobago rum, which shall be sold for the most they will bring. These are at the service of the state. If we succeed, I shall be remunerated; if not, they will be of no use to me. We can raise a brigade; and our friend Stark, who so nobly sustained the honor of our arms at Bunker Hill, may safely be entrusted with the command, *and we will check Burgoyne.*"

John Stark, farmer, was sent for. He stood up before the Assembly and gave his answer. Yes, he would raise a brigade of New Hampshire men, and he would "stop Burgoyne." But he would not answer to the commander in chief of the northern Continental army. He would run his own campaign and answer to New Hampshire alone.

All right, said the Assembly. Raise your own men. Find your own battle field. Fight your own battle. We will make you a brigadier general. They did and he was off. His popularity in New Hampshire was very great. More men came than he wanted but he took them all, and sent them to join with the Green Mountain Boys at Manchester, Vermont.

When the Continental Congress in Philadelphia heard of Stark's independent command, they disapproved strongly and sent him an immediate order to conform to the rules, and at once. He paid no attention to this censure and command, but went straight ahead on his own way. As a man under a remote order, he might have been a failure in this difficult assignment. Left to himself and given complete freedom, he was ready for anything. Burgoyne's army was on the way, collecting horses, oxen, cattle, and military supplies along the frontier. Colonel Baum's section of this army was ahead, and these were the men Stark's force would meet. Some of Baum's men were Indians.

As fast as his volunteers arrived, Stark sent them in companies to various points. Colonel Warner went to Manchester. Stark headed for Bennington. With some fifteen hundred men under his command, wet to the skin from rain that had poured all night and the next morning, he divided his troops into three divisions, keeping the reserve for himself. At three o'clock he attacked Baum on three sides.

PORTSMOUTH

Just before the first shots were fired, according to the memory of several witnesses, General Stark stood before his men and spoke two sentences:

"There, my boys, are the red-coats and Tories. You must beat them or Molly Stark sleeps a widow tonight."

Words like these from a leader in the moment of battle, make men do the impossible, and Molly Stark did not sleep a widow that night. These soldiers in working clothes, each man with a husk of corn in his hat to distinguish him from a Tory, also in his working clothes, had won one of the more important battles of the war. Colonel Baum had been killed, and also most of his officers, two hundred and twenty-six of his men, and seven hundred taken prisoner. Stark had lost four officers, ten privates, and had forty-two wounded.

The victory was important because it stopped Baum, the advance unit of Burgoyne's army. Burgoyne's surrender was one of the further sequels to it, and also an end to danger on the northern frontier. For New Hampshire land forces to have proved so effective discouraged Britain from thinking she could quickly subdue the colonies by land attacks. Her navy was queen of the seas and America had no navy at all. The emphasis from now on would be by sea. General Stark was made a member of the council stipulating the surrender of Burgoyne. This seemed almost like a pardon for his obstinacy in insisting that he run his own campaign. At least in the Bennington victory he won a front rank place among New Hampshire heroes.

ᴥ8ᴫ

"I Have Not Yet Begun to Fight"

WITH THE British land forces checked and the battle on the sea begun, Portsmouth was more wide-awake than ever. As a seaport she would be in danger of attack and invasion. She was also one of the colonies to supply men who knew the sea and were trained to handle ships. Every man and boy in the town was at home on the water. Every family had a boat of some sort, and some member of each family had some skill that belongs to boats or sailing. The shipyard on Seavey's Island in the harbor could use it all. Nor would it surprise anyone that Portsmouth would claim one of the great naval heroes of the war. He was none other than John Paul Jones. He was not a native Portsmouth boy or even a native American. He was a Scot whose story is one of America's great hero tales.

He was born on the shore of the Irish sea where a long arm of it, called the Solway Firth, washes up between

England and Scotland. In clear weather he could see the shore of England. On the other side Ireland was a little farther away. Straight ahead was the sea that was his boyhood world. It would be his world for life.

His father was a gardener on an estate called Arbigland. The family name was not Jones, but Paul, and the boy was given the father's name, John Paul. He gave himself the name Jones when he was a young man, apparently to conceal his identity, for he was in trouble. There were an older brother, two older sisters, and one younger sister. The five children grew up in a stone cottage with the seashore as their playground. John Paul knew the ways of wind and wave from the time he knew anything, and he could manage a rowboat to the admiration of the fisher folk when he was a very small boy. The fishermen were his boyhood friends and often his companions. They took him out of sight of land almost from the time he was old enough to walk. He could not remember a time when the sea was strange to him. Ships of all sizes, bound for far places—sloops, brigs, schooners—were always on his horizon. He knew the names of many of them, their ports of call, their masters.

When he was thirteen years old, healthy and strong, he left the stone cottage and went to sea as a ship's boy. This was in 1761. He was the youngest on board the little packet sloop, the *Friendship*, which was going to the Barbados in the West Indies with a heavy cargo. His father signed papers of apprenticeship, which would mean seven years on shipboard while his son learned to be a sailor. This was exactly what John Paul wanted more than anything else in the world. He packed his first sea chest, said good-bye to Solway Firth for at least six months, and was off.

There were twenty-eight in the crew of this small ship, and as ship's boy he would serve Captain Nelson and the mates, do small chores everywhere on the ship. Best of all, he would learn, as for uncounted hours he watched the sailors and connected the shouted orders with their skill of hand and speed of action. He came to feel at home in storm or calm, as one emergency after another tested the nerve and skill of all on board. No training on a practice ship, safe in the harbor, could have done this for him. The *Friendship* was on a real voyage, with a real cargo and a harbor to find across these unending miles. He was with men who knew how to find it, and he could learn also. When the ship anchored in the Barbados, he had learned more than in any other two months of his life up to this time, possibly more than in any two months yet to come.

After leaving the Barbados with its cargo exchanged, the *Friendship* sailed up the Rappahannock River to Hampton, Virginia, near where John Paul's brother, William, was living in the town of Fredericksburg. He was a tailor, and this summer visit, while the ship's cargo was again being exchanged, was a touch of home for John Paul. Virginia meant also an introduction to a new way of life in an altogether new country, "my favorite country from the age of thirteen," he wrote later. Virginia, in 1761, was not yet greatly changed from the unbroken forest it had been when Captain John Smith first saw it. To a boy who had grown up on a sandy beach it was a land of almost unreal beauty, and he determined at once that someday it would be his home. He found joy in dreaming this dream, and this was a summer never to be forgotten.

While the *Friendship,* laden with hogsheads of rum and barrels of sugar from Barbados, was being unloaded and filled again with a new cargo of tobacco, pig iron, and barrel staves for Whitehaven, England, John Paul learned much more that was new to him from listening to the talk of the Virginia customers in his brother's tailor shop. These Virginia gentlemen knew things he had never heard of. Even their strange accents gave him a new ambition. He would like to talk like a gentleman too. How did one begin? The summer also brought books to read and John Paul discovered new excitements on the printed page. All his life afterward, on land or sea, he was a reader and a student, for he was never in school again.

On October 5, the *Friendship* weighed anchor and began the long sail back to Whitehaven; two more months to learn in sterner weathers. December meant Christmas at home for John Paul. He had had nearly a year of new experiences. It had been a year which had initiated him into the seaman's life and given him a brief glimpse into the lives of gentlemen. He wanted to live in both worlds. The summer in Virginia had given him a new purpose, as he continued to follow the rough and dangerous life of the sea. He would be an American.

He made two more round trips with Captain Nelson as an apprenticed ship's boy to Barbados and Virginia, and he did his work so well that when the *Friendship* was sold in

1764, he was released from the remaining four years of his apprenticeship. Not many boys of sixteen had made such records. This early release meant the end of working for nothing. He was now free to take an assignment for pay on any ship that had a vacancy for him. Had he been older and wiser, he might have chosen differently, but he was impatient to begin, and took an offer as third mate on the *King George,* a ship sailing out of Whitehaven and carrying slaves to the West Indies.

After two more years he changed ships and became chief mate on another slave ship plying between Africa and Jamaica. It was a British ship, only fifty feet long and carrying seventy-seven Negroes below deck. This was an experience John Paul could not endure and when the ship reached Jamaica, he asked for a discharge. While he waited for a chance to get back to England, the ship *John,* with Captain Samuel McAdam from his own home corner of Solway Firth, arrived in Jamaica. A free passage home was offered and of course John Paul took it. On this passage, a deadly fever broke out on the ship, and both master and mate died. Who would navigate this sixty-ton ship home? John Paul's chance had come. He had studied navigation by the stars since he first had embarked with Captain Nelson and he felt confident that he could do it. He took the challenge and brought the ship *John* safely back to his own village of Kirkcudbright.

The reward, which need not surprise us, was that he was made master of this small ship on her next voyage to the American continent. Boyhood ended with the appointment.

He was a man now, with authority over other men and with responsibility for the safety of all on board. Those who knew him said that the power to command seemed to be natural to him. There was authority in a mere gesture of his hand and in his voice. He spoke low, even softly in conversation, but when he gave an order, it was in tones that left the hearer nothing to do but obey at once. Now he could use that power, and with no one over him. He was not a tall man, at his full growth only five feet five inches, but he was straight as an Indian. When he gave a command, his height, his companions said, seemed to increase and his quickness of movement made him seem everywhere at once. He was always very carefully dressed, with a sword in his belt, and authority seemed to walk the decks as he passed.

Had he known that authority was enough and held his temper in times of impatience or anger, his story as a ship-master might have been clear of blots, but as a young man he was not yet wise enough for that. Once when the ship's carpenter, Mungo Maxwell, refused to obey an order, he had him lashed with a cat-o'-nine-tails on his bare back. This punishment was too much for Mungo Maxwell's pride, and when the ship reached Tobago, he made a complaint against its master and joined another crew. Ordinarily, nothing would have come of this routine complaint, but it so happened that on his next ship Mungo Maxwell died of fever, and when John Paul reached the Solway Firth on his return, he found himself charged with the death of this man. He was legally cleared of the charge, for of course he was not to blame for the man's death from fever, but the charge was never forgotten by his boyhood neighbors.

Soon there was another more serious charge, this time the death of a slave who had run against John Paul's sword during another moment of discipline on shipboard. John Paul was cleared of intended injury in this case, but his record as a commander would always be darkened by the outbursts of anger back of both of them.

After the second episode, which had taken place on the ship *Betsy,* there are two years of mystery during which John Paul disappeared from ship records. He came back in 1775, when he was twenty-eight years old, no longer John Paul, but John Paul Jones, the name by which the world knows him. He had added the Jones himself, probably for concealment during the black period when he feared revenge from friends of the man he had accidentally killed. He had also during those two years become a citizen of the colony of Virginia.

It was nine years from his first independent command of the ship *John* until he came to Portsmouth to command the *Ranger,* her most famous ship of Revolutionary days. Those nine years had been historic years for the thirteen colonies. The feeling toward England had changed for many hundreds of Americans. The determination to be free was no longer held secret. Every colony was getting ready.

After Lexington and Concord made history in 1775, it was open war. The Continental Congress in Philadelphia named George Washington commander in chief of the Continental army, an army which hardly yet existed. Esek Hopkins was made commander in chief of the Continental navy, which also hardly existed. There were only four ships under its command, the two frigates *Alfred* and *Columbus,* and the two brigs *Cabot* and *Andrew Doria.* The *Alfred* was the largest of these and had twenty nine-pound guns.

John Paul Jones lost no time in getting a naval post. As soon as he heard of the appointment of a naval commander, he hastened to Philadelphia and applied for a commission. On December 7, 1775, he was made first lieutenant in the Continental navy and assigned to the *Alfred,* her largest ship. His orders were to pursue British merchant ships but not to sink them. Hostilities had begun and there was no time to build ships. America needed every ship she could get, and by the capture of good merchant ships, she might assemble a working navy in a short time.

Pirates and privateers had been seizing merchant ships on all waters for generations, selling their cargo, and distributing the money among the crew. John Paul Jones and his fellow masters of merchant ships were being pirates for their country. The colonies had two thousand privateers engaged in seizing merchant ships at this time, under authority of the Continental Congress. Ships were being added by this means day after day. No wonder Europe called them pirates. They were nothing else in method.

After five months as lieutenant on the *Alfred,* John Paul Jones was given the temporary rank of captain, with orders to annoy British shipping around Bermuda. With an armed

ship, a crew of seventy men, and a free hand, he set forth
on one of the most fortunate cruises of his life. In forty-nine
days he took seven vessels, and on a second cruise into
northern waters repeated his success with somewhat more
difficulty. After these two successes, he had hoped to be
made commander of a fleet, but in this he was disappointed. Instead, by order of the Congress, he was directed
to command the new sloop, the *Ranger,* which was being
built at Portsmouth. For many months the men, women, and
children of this city of harbors, warehouses, rope walks, seamen, and families of seamen, had watched every step in
the long construction of this ship that was their own, from
keel to masts, to rigging, to every yard of cordage made in
their own rope walks. They greeted John Paul Jones, the
new commander of this beautiful square-rigger, as their own
special hero even before he had set foot on board for the
first time. A young man could hardly have hoped for more
thrilling acceptance. He was welcomed as though he were a
veteran of many years, and he was only twenty-eight. His
handsome appearance, charm, and gentlemanly manners
delighted this aristocratic town, and from the moment he
arrived, all doors were thrown open to him.

Ranger was still a bare ship, and for many days he
directed every step of her furnishing and equipping. It took
him three months to rig her, store her with provisions, and
find the men to man her. His handbill used in recruiting
sailors called for "Gentlemen Seamen and able-bodied
Landsmen who wish to distinguish themselves in the GLO-

RIOUS CAUSE of their country and make their fortune." A drum and a fife in the streets and colors flying helped enlistment, and a crew was soon assembled.

Just as sailing time came, the news of Burgoyne's surrender at Saratoga filled the Continental forces with new hope and sudden joy. John Paul Jones's orders were suddenly changed. He would sail at once to carry news of this surrender to Benjamin Franklin in Paris. A proud voyage indeed this would be. His "gentlemen seamen" were chosen and as he sailed out of the mouth of the Piscataqua as commander of this new and beautiful ship, with the whole town watching, he could hardly have hoped for a greater triumph. A second ship made the French coast first, as John Paul Jones went off his course to capture two small merchant ships on the way, but his meeting with Benjamin Franklin was no less a pleasure because of this delay. Franklin was fifty years older than this ambitious young captain, but each man was willing to listen to the other, and a friendship began which lasted many years.

John Paul Jones was next ordered to cruise around English shores and annoy English shipping. What he did accomplished very little in terms of military success, but he made his name known throughout England and kept men wondering what he might do next. His idea was to do something unexpected and therefore to catch the enemy off guard. The result was to put English ships on watch for him everywhere, but never in the right place. Pirate Jones, as they called him, would always be somewhere else, doing what no one else had thought of doing in the name of war-

The Ranger *receiving the salute to the Stars and Stripes by the French Squadron in Quiberon Bay, February 14, 1778. A proud moment for John Paul Jones.*

fare. By this method he made news, if not history, whatever he did.

First came the salute to the Stars and Stripes in Quiberon Bay, a brief but important item in American naval history. A large number of French ships were in this harbor, one of them the flagship of an admiral of the fleet. The Stars and

Stripes had been authorized as the American flag by the Continental Congress only shortly before, on June 14, 1777. As yet there had not been an official salute by a foreign power. John Paul Jones saw his chance and sent a message to the French Admiral, asking for a gun-by-gun salute. When the answer came back that only nine guns would be fired, he was disappointed; but even so, this was an honor not to be missed. This would be the first salute to the new flag. The guns were fired, and a new page in American naval history was written.

The flag that John Paul Jones was flying on the *Ranger* was probably the Grand Union flag, seven red and six white stripes, with thirteen white stars on the blue field in the upper left-hand corner. Before the Declaration of Independence, the Union Jack with the crosses of St. George and St. Stephen in the upper left-hand corner had usually been flown by American ships. The yellow flag with a coiled serpent and the inscription DON'T TREAD ON ME had often been carried by regiments and ships. There were various other designs, but after June 14, 1777, the Stars and Stripes was the chosen symbol. The official salute by the French flagship, which Captain Jones had been bold enough to invite, helped to make it recognized as the national flag.

His next news item was the young man's bolder idea. He decided to carry out his orders by making a night raid on Whitehaven harbor, the English port from which he had first taken to sea as a ship's boy. A whole fleet of English ships was there. He could not hope to conquer them in a sea fight, but he could humiliate them in a night raid. He planned well. In the darkness of a foggy night he went ashore with two small parties in rowboats. With his own hands he disabled the cannons of ship after ship by driving spikes into the vents so that they could not be fired. He also threw inflammable material on board.

Had it not been for a traitor among his own men, who had gone ashore in one of the rowboats and alerted people near the docks, more ships might have been damaged. Excited officers and seamen were quickly aroused and ran back to shore to find their ships blazing. John Paul Jones and his accomplices, all but the traitor, got away before they were pursued, and went back to the *Ranger* in the darkness. The harbor fires were put out, but all England rang with the news of what Pirate Jones had dared and accomplished. The British navy was humiliated, and it did little good to call the American captain names. His own name was now widely known throughout the English nation, and what would he do next?

Two miles away the next morning, a squad of sailors from the *Ranger* landed at St. Mary's Isle, and walked up the path to the castle of the Earl of Selkirk. John Paul Jones's intent this time was to capture the Earl, take him as hostage, and hold him until Britain released the American sailors in British prisons. There were many of them. The plan might have worked, but when the squad reached the castle they were told that the Earl was away from home. The sailors were angry, for now there would be no ransom money for them. When they returned to the *Ranger,* John Paul Jones sent them back again to take the Selkirk silver, but to do it politely and do no harm to Lady Selkirk. Not exactly what a Countess might expect from a rebellious colony in America, but being helpless, she delivered the silver. The teapot and coffeepot were in use and the butler hid them, but Lady Selkirk commanded him to deliver them also.

Unexpectedly, for he was always doing the unexpected, John Paul Jones personally bought the silver from the sailors for $600 of his own money, divided the money among them, and sent the silver back to Lady Selkirk with a polite letter of apology. The story is told that the tea leaves from morning breakfast in the castle were still in the pot when it was returned. A trivial incident, all of it, in international affairs, but the story went all over England, and once again people said, What kind of man is this John Paul Jones? A pirate who is also a gentleman.

But he could also be a fighter. Almost immediately after the St. Mary's Isle affair, he took the British sloop of war *Drake* off Belfast Lough, killed the captain, and took one hundred and thirty-three men prisoners. It was out of this spectacular victory that the best known of various John Paul Jones ballads was written. It began:

> "You have heard o' Paul Jones
> Have you not? Have you not?
> And you've heard o' Paul Jones
> Have you not?"

Certainly. Everybody had. A privateer and a pirate, said the newspapers. A hero, said the man in the street. The bold attack on Whitehaven, the carrying off of a lady's silver and then sending it back again were news of another sort. Both escapades created fear, and now the *Drake* had been taken. What next?

The next event was to be the great battle of John Paul's life—not a mere skirmish or a sensational surprise this time —but a major battle on the sea. It was the fight of the *Bon Homme Richard* and the British *Serapis* off the English coast of Flamborough Head on September 23, 1779. John Paul Jones had waited three months for a new command, hoping it might be a French ship with French soldiers. Lafayette on land and John Paul Jones on sea against Britain seemed a very good plan to some leaders, Benjamin Franklin among them, but this plan did not win approval in the end. Instead Jones was named commander of a fleet of five vessels, with the *Bon Homme Richard* as his own ship. This vessel had formerly been called *Le Duc Duras.* It was purchased by America and renamed by John Paul Jones *Bon Homme Richard,* in translation of Franklin's title, *Poor Richard.* Everybody was reading Franklin's book at the time, and Franklin himself was one of the most popular men in France. This name pleased the French as much as the Americans. There was almost magic in it.

Getting all five ships ready for battle was a long assignment. John Paul Jones liked equipping a ship almost as well as fighting in it, and he went to work with enthusiasm and energy. *Bon Homme Richard* was the largest ship he had ever commanded and she needed nearly everything done for her, chiefly providing cannon and space for soldiers as well as space for her sailors. The four supporting ships were *Alliance, Pallas, Vengeance,* and *Le Cerf.* By courtesy Jones was called commander of this fleet, but by act of the Continental Congress he was still only a captain in rank.

His officers were mainly American, but his crew were English, Portuguese, Irish, and a sprinkling of other European nationalities. Few of them spoke or understood English.

All England was watching the preparations on this ship. "The squadron of John Paul Jones," it was called, as it was sighted here and there after leaving port. Ballads began to be printed again, with news in them.

"You've heard that amazement has fill'd all the coast,
  Since the tidings of Jones by last Wednesday's post."

It was more than amazement. There was fear of his very name, rebel and pirate that he was still called. It might not be merely a nuisance raid this time.

He headed for Newcastle upon Tyne with the thought of blockading the port from which England's coal supply was coming. He knew that the frigate *Serapis,* brand new and heavily armed, was in the neighborhood. She was escorting a large merchant convoy and he was on the lookout for her. In the early afternoon of September 22, he sighted her escorting some forty-one ships along the coast. His chance had come.

Captain Pearson of the *Serapis* had been warned. He knew that John Paul Jones was at hand. Presently he could see the *Bon Homme Richard* and three of the smaller ships close to her. John Paul Jones could see the *Serapis* and one ship near her. Her convoy would be a great prize, for it carried military supplies the Americans needed.

Just as the sun was setting, for this was to be a night battle, he gave the order, "Form Line of Battle." Two of his fleet, the *Alliance* and *Pallas,* instead of obeying, sailed away. They were probably afraid of *Serapis.* *Vengeance* watched from a distance. Where was *Le Cerf?* Not even in sight. *Richard* would do battle alone against this newer, larger, better equipped frigate. The two ships came alongside, *Richard* flying the Union Jack to mislead Captain Pearson. This was a common practice. Captain Pearson hailed, "What ship is that?" Not hearing an answer, he hailed again, "Answer immediately, or I shall be under the necessity of firing upon you."

At this point John Paul Jones ran up the red, white, and blue ensign and gave the order to fire. *Serapis* answered with fire and the battle was on. Almost immediately two of the *Bon Homme Richard*'s guns burst, killing men and blowing up part of the deck on the side toward the *Serapis.* Without guns on that side, John Paul Jones knew that he would be lost. The ships were less than one hundred feet apart. Each of them was already afire in several places.

John Paul Jones's strategy was to get his bow across the stern or the bow of his enemy. This would have to be a hand-to-hand fight. He must also get close enough so that the guns of the *Serapis* could not operate. *Serapis* tried exactly the same strategy, aiming at *Richard*'s bow. In a minute *Richard*'s stern was directly across the bow of *Serapis.* It was a most dangerous position.

"Has your ship struck?" Captain Pearson called out, meaning, "Do you surrender?" Not John Paul Jones. "No, I have not yet begun to fight," he called back, not in his soft drawing room voice, but in a tone that made every man of his crew as strong as two men; and they began in that minute to prove it.

The *Serapis* tried to get clear, but a sudden wind sent her first midway into *Richard*'s side and then straight alongside, bow to stern and stern to bow. The muzzles of one ship's guns struck the muzzles of the other's.

"Well done, my brave lads," John Paul Jones called out, and gave the order to grapple the ships together with hooks. With his own hands he helped to make the hooks fast in that perilous moment. He was unprotected from gunfire. The hooks held.

Captain Pearson ordered the hooks unfastened, but *Richard*'s men fired at every man who came near them.

Suddenly the harvest moon came out from behind a cloud bank. This is one of the most peaceful sights that nature gives us, but on the night of September 23, 1779, instead of looking down on a calm sea or on quiet fields with songs of the woodthrush and chirp of crickets in the air, the moon looked down on a battle to the death on the sea. For two more hours the two crews held out. Men were dying. Both ships were on fire.

John Paul Jones helped to roll one of the guns to the opposite side of the deck and manned it himself. He aimed every shot steadily at the mainmast of the *Serapis*. One of his men, high in *Richard*'s topmast, crawled out on a spar, lay down flat, and took careful aim. He had a grenade in his hand. Slowly he raised his arm and threw the grenade directly through one of the hatches of *Serapis,* causing an explosion which ran like a chain along the deck as cartridges set in a row exploded. Death, destruction, and a fire which threatened the whole ship followed. But John Paul Jones kept right on shooting at the mainmast of his enemy. In a moment of exhaustion, he fell back. The situation seemed desperate.

"Captain, for God's sake, strike," one of his own men called out, seeing his great danger.

"No. I will sink," he answered, "I will never strike." And he loaded the gun again. Another sailor came with the word that there was already five feet of water in the hold.

"Release the prisoners and set them to helping with the pumps," was the order in answer. Not only on fire, but sinking. He had only three cannon left. Another of his men, an officer, implored him to "strike," but he kept right on pelting at the *Serapis,* straight at her mainmast.

At 10:30 P.M. as the moon shone on, the battered mainmast began to waver. That was the zero moment for Captain Pearson, although he was not sinking. He gave the order for his men to cease fire. Lieutenant Dale of the *Richard* boarded the *Serapis.* *Richard*'s shooting stopped.

Lieutenant Dale conducted Captain Pearson aboard the *Richard* and introduced him to John Paul Jones. Captain Pearson handed over his sword. John Paul Jones returned it, and spoke a word of praise for Captain Pearson's brave fight, then invited him below for a glass of wine in his cabin. The courtesy of naval leaders has few equals. The fight was over.

After three and a half hours of fighting both ships were in sad condition, the *Bon Homme Richard*'s much the worse. She was hurt mainly below the water line, the *Serapis* mainly above it. Obviously the *Richard* could not stay afloat many hours, although her surviving crew struggled bravely to save her, manning her pumps for thirty-six hours without stop-

Sea fight of the Bon Homme Richard *and the* Serapis *off Flamborough Head, September 23, 1779.*

ping. But in spite of their struggle, the water in the hold deepened and after another whole day and night, John Paul Jones was convinced there was no hope the ship could be saved. The wounded and the prisoners were transferred to the *Serapis* and to the other ships in the fleet. No one of these had helped at all in the fight. In fact, the *Alliance* at one point had pulled alongside and shot directly at the *Richard*. One hopes it was a mistake, although the evidence would seem to be otherwise.

Captain Jones took down his flag and gave order to his men to ABANDON SHIP. It was 10:00 P.M. of the second night. Once more the moon looked on. At 4:00 A.M. of September 25, pumps were stopped and the last man left the ship. At 10 in the morning the hull of the *Bon Homme Richard* dipped and she slowly disappeared, as her captain and crew looked on. There is no sadder moment for shipmen.

The *Bon Homme Richard* was gone, but even in that moment John Paul Jones had to act quickly. British ships were on the way. They would pursue him, as they did, but he escaped. He had fought the greatest battle of his life on the sea and written a victory for American power there as it had earlier been written for the land forces.

The British press still denounced him as a pirate, but not all the British people agreed. He was the kind of man and had fought the kind of fight that makes a man a hero even to his enemies. The most popular ballad about him gained many new stanzas.

> "You have heard of Paul Jones, have you not?
> Have you not?
>
> He took the *Serapis*
> Did he not, did he not?

He took the *Serapis,* tho' the battle was hot;
But a rogue and a vagabond
    Is he not?"

But they sang it now with a ringing admiration. There were more ballads, more crowds following when he came to land after his return to France. It was a long chapter of admiration. For a brief time he was almost as popular as Benjamin Franklin himself.

"Here comes Paul Jones, such a nice fellow!
  His ship went down at England's end.
  Here comes Paul Jones; such a nice fellow!
  A born American; no Englishman at all."

Ballads sing the praises of a brave man, even if they have him born in the wrong country. In his letters after this victory, John Paul Jones left off the John and afterward signed himself, Paul Jones. No one knows why.

He grew impatient during the long autumn and winter while the *Serapis* was being made seaworthy again. Finally the French agreed to take over the entire squadron, except the *Alliance,* and Paul Jones transferred his flag to her staff, went to Paris, and stayed while she was being fitted for the voyage to America. He was the hero of all classes and enjoyed his brief day to the full. Benjamin Franklin introduced him at court; he was presented to King Louis XVI. Artists painted his portrait. Many who had expected, at the receptions in his honor, to greet a rough sailor were amazed at his soft-speech, his courtly ways—as though he had spent all his life with men and women of polite society. His thirteen-year-old ambition to grow up to be a gentleman, which had begun while he listened to a conversation in his brother's Virginia tailor shop, was now a fact.

His greatest honor was a decoration from the French king, the Order of Military Merit, which entitled him to be called Chevalier. Honors by a foreign government were forbidden to American military men without the permission of the Continental Congress, but to Paul Jones's great happiness, this permission was granted, and he proudly wore the eight-pointed gold star suspended by a blue ribbon from his buttonhole. There were fleurs-de-lis in the angles and a motto, *Pro Virtute Bellico*—for bravery in war. He wears this emblem in the famous bust of him made by the French sculptor, Houdon. The king also gave him a gold-hilted sword bearing in Latin the inscription: *Louis XVI rewards the Stout Vindicator of the Freedom of the Seas.* This sword today stands near Paul Jones's tomb in the crypt of the Naval Academy at Annapolis, where his body lies.

This pleasant interval of glory and honor in Paris took many weeks. The war was coming into its last chapters when Paul Jones arrived in America more than two years after his great victory. He had been promised, as reward from America, the command of the largest ship yet built in the American navy. This was the *America,* then being built at Portsmouth. Not knowing that this command was never to be, Paul Jones hastened back from Philadelphia, in 1781, to another round of honor in this port city which claimed him as

JOHN PAUL JONES *by Jean Antoine Houdon. This bust stands on the first landing of the main stairway in the John Paul Jones House, Portsmouth.*

COAT OF ARMS *made by John Paul Jones. No doubt the making of this crest grew out of his young ambition to be a gentleman in spite of his humble birth. Instead of the usual symbols of heraldry, he found symbols in his own life.*

one of their own. During this pleasant stay he lived in the house which is now called by his name, in the room which has that name scratched on its window pane, probably by Paul Jones himself.

Finishing and equipping the *America* took so much time that he began to be worried over the promised assignment as its captain. Well he might be. There was jealousy of him and criticism, some of it deserved, but he still hoped for the ship. His hopes were disappointed. In midsummer, 1782, a French fleet of thirteen ships convoyed by *Le Magnifique* attempted to make Boston harbor. *Le Magnifique* struck a reef and was severely damaged. Congress immediately paid a long debt of gratitude to the French nation by giving her the new-built *America,* the proudest ship of the new nation, just as she was ready to be launched. The war was nearly over and there might not have been a chance for another great naval victory. On the day the proud ship *America* was launched, John Paul Jones stood at his post and gave the orders which guided her safely down the ways. All five thousand Portsmouth residents watched from the shore.

John Paul Jones did not have another ship. His day of naval glory was over. One great battle and a victory to end it had won him a place in history. He had written a bright page, not only in the Portsmouth story but in American annals of the sea. Today every American naval officer and every bluejacket knows those seven words, spoken when his ship was on fire and more than half of her guns silenced. "I have not yet begun to fight," he said, and went on to victory.

∼9∽

George Washington
Pays a Visit

PORTSMOUTH remembers triumphs of peace as well as celebrations of victory in war on land or sea. When the Revolution was over and George Washington had been chosen first
President of the new nation, he paid Portsmouth the honor of
a four-day visit. He wanted, he said, "to visit every part of
the United States," to become better acquainted with her
people and particularly to know how they felt about the new
government. Every president since Washington has made
similar tours for the same reasons, but there is no time like
the first time. For Portsmouth it was a visit no resident in
1789 would ever forget. They talked of these four days for
years afterward.

Washington had been inaugurated on April 30. He was
in New York during the first session of the Congress which
closed September 29. He consulted with other leaders as to
the wisdom of the trip, for he had been ill. They all approved

and he made preparations. He set out from New York on October 13, expecting to be absent for one month. Two secretaries and six servants went with him. Our knowledge of what happened comes in part from Washington's own personal diary, which he kept by the day, and in part from New Hampshire newspapers, the *Spy* and the *Gazette*. All that these newspapers had to say in those days appeared on a single sheet of paper folded twice, making eight pages. Items of news were usually a single sentence.

It took nine days for the party to go from New York to Boston, and until two days before he arrived, Portsmouth did not know the precise day on which to expect him. Progress was slow, for roads were rough and streams had to be forded at many points. Advance notice came by post riders. Back and forth these messengers rode between Boston and Portsmouth, keeping the town in touch with the slow advance. Wayside greetings often caused delay. On October 29, the *Spy* announced that beyond a doubt, President Washington would be there the second day afterward, as he was.

At the New Hampshire state line he was met by the president of the state, John Sullivan, by the officer of the day, by Senators, and by other officials. He had been escorted to this point by Massachusetts officials and troops of cavalry. Good-byes were said, Massachusetts troops wheeled, and New Hampshire officials with seven hundred cavalry replaced them as escort. Washington had been riding in a coach. He stepped down, was introduced to the welcoming officials, and mounted his white horse. Mounted, he reviewed the New Hampshire troops, noting with pleasure their red and white

uniforms made from materials of New Hampshire manufacture.

The review over, he took his place again in the carriage
and the procession moved forward. Along the way, from
single farmhouses, or neighborhoods with a cluster of houses,
men, women, and children were waiting to see him pass.

As he neared the outskirts of Portsmouth and the cavalcade
was sighted, bells began to ring, cannons boomed, everyone
cheered. The whole town was waiting. The tradesmen and
workers were lined up on both sides of Congress Street,
grouped alphabetically according to their occupations—
baker, blacksmith, carpenter, and on down to painter,
weaver. Every door and window was crowded. All the
schoolchildren were in line, every school wearing a different-
colored cap and every cap adorned with a diamond-shaped
cockade and a feather.

The procession headed toward the State House in the
center of the Parade. From the door on Congress Street, the
President was escorted through the building to the Senate
Chamber, which opened onto the balcony. As the balcony
door opened and he appeared before the whole town, which
was massed just below, a great shout went up in welcome.
At just that moment there was an echoing salute from Fort
William and Mary, and the ships in the harbor broke out
their colors.

President Washington was then introduced as the "man
who has given birth to the Empire of America." The town
band played, and from a platform that had been erected just
opposite the balcony, a town chorus sang three odes which

had been composed by a citizen of Portsmouth. The first verse
of one of them begins:

> "Behold he comes! Columbia's pride,
>   And nature's boast, her fav'rite son,
>   Of valor, wisdom, Truth well Try'd
>   Hail, Matchless Washington!"

After the singing of the odes in his honor, Washington stood
on the balcony and reviewed the troops as they marched past,
the town tradesmen walking two by two behind them. He
was then escorted to Brewster's Coffee House and Tavern,
Portsmouth's best in those days. That evening he entertained
at dinner the Portsmouth town leaders and the men who
had been delegates to the Convention which drafted the
Federal Constitution. Codfish was on the dinner menu, of
course. After dinner he drank tea at the Langdon House, a
few steps away, and returned to his lodgings for an early
bedtime. Very probably he did not see the thirteen rockets
and other fireworks that were shot off in his honor from the
State House balcony.

The next day was Sunday and of course he went to church:
it was Queen's Chapel in the morning and Old North Congregational meetinghouse in the afternoon. He was dressed,
we are told, in a black velvet suit with black silk stockings.
Both churches were crowded far beyond their usual congre-
gations, and every hitching post, every tree, had a saddle
horse tied—most of them also with pillions behind the saddle,
so that the wife could ride, perhaps with a baby in her arms.

Country wagons and city carriages were along the streets. The congregation included men in powdered wigs, embroidered waistcoats, ruffles, cocked hats. Some of them also carried gold- or silver-headed canes. Their ladies were dressed in robes of fashion with bonnets and plumes to match. There were also men and women, far the greater number, clad in homespun garments of their own weaving.

Sunday ended with Washington's writing letters and entering the day's events in his diary.

On Monday morning he took an excursion down the river, apparently an event not announced to the public, or the river would have been too crowded. Many watched from the shore. He was in a boat rowed by seamen clothed in white, and followed by one with seamen clothed in blue. The town band furnished the music. At the Fort of William and Mary the cannon fired a thirteen-gun salute. Washington's diary reports that after passing the fort, the party went on to the fishing banks and fished for cod. The tide was not right for success at this hour and only two fish were caught. Tradition says that one of the party, seeing that the President had caught nothing and having a fish on his own line, handed it to him so that Washington drew in the fish. This detail may be fiction, and also the following one, that the President handed out a dollar in exchange. Such, however, is the story.

On the way back the boat landed briefly at the house built by Colonel Wentworth, whose widow, once a serving maid in his house, was hostess this day to the President of the united colonies. A truly American story, as we like to believe.

PORTSMOUTH

In the afternoon on Monday, the Portsmouth people assembled again before the State House balcony to hear the address of the town to George Washington and his reply. Both speeches were brief, the President's only four paragraphs long. There was no loudspeaker. The whole town could gather near enough to hear every word. Tea drinking at the Langdon House ended this important day.

On Tuesday the President sat for his portrait by a Boston artist who had been refused in Boston, but had followed the party to Portsmouth for another chance. The sitting over, Washington did something that pleased the town very much. He paid a call on the mother of Tobias Lear, the Portsmouth boy who after his graduation from Harvard had been employed as tutor to Washington's two adopted children, Patsy and Jackie, and now was one of his private secretaries. The President walked down Hunking Street to Mrs. Lear's home, bringing gifts sent by Martha Washington. He held Mrs. Lear's little daughter, aged five, on his knee—a fact she remembered all her life. The youngest child was baptized during this call, and of course no one need ask the name given him. As Washington laid his hand on the baby's head, he said he hoped this boy would be "a better man than the one whose name he bears." Naval records tell us that he grew up to be a commander.

After dinner in the evening with officials in the Assembly room and an "elegant ball" afterward, the festivities which Portsmouth had planned through many weeks for her famous guest were over. The ball was remembered as a successful ending to the four-day celebration. Cuffee Whipple, a Negro, had "fiddled the dances" and all was gay. No one reported whether Washington danced, but very probably he did. He remarked on the beauty of the Portsmouth ladies and noted especially the blackness of their hair, as compared with southern ladies, a compliment that they remembered happily.

On Wednesday morning Washington departed without fanfare, according to his own wish. These had been four memorable days in Portsmouth history. Other high-ranking visitors of state would come to Portsmouth through the years and share the hospitality of her people. The list is long and notable, but it is a list in which the name of George Washington is still first, in honor as well as in time.

~⁓10⁓~

A City Takes Her Place

AT THE TIME of George Washington's visit in 1789, Portsmouth could look back over more than a century and a half of history. She had been one of the earliest American settlements and a part of the New England story since the beginning. She was now a growing town of five thousand people and her sternest pioneer days were behind her. She had lived through the time when her streets were narrow paths bordered by strawberry patches. Her first houses had only two rooms on the ground floor, the kitchen and the parents' bedroom. The children slept in a row on the attic floor. Life was simpler in those days than it would ever be again—harder too, perhaps, and often dangerous, but not unhappy.

By the time President Washington came, many things had changed. Portsmouth had found her place in the America of her time. It was a place in many ways different from that of her inland neighbors. She was a port, fronting the ocean on New Hampshire's fourteen miles of the Atlantic. The open sea was her eastern doorway. It was a doorway wide open to the world on the other side of the Atlantic, a door she could not have shut, even if she had desired. With this door wide open she could never be what we call provincial. She would be a city of ships, of wide-stretching wharves, of trade, of far voyages. Her ships would sail the world's waters. Europe would be her market place. In the days of sailing ships she was two days nearer Europe than Boston. She would be a port of call and a landing place for travelers from the other side of the world.

From her earliest days her workmen had built canoes, river boats, and small merchant ships for coastwise trade. They would build larger and larger ships for ocean crossing. The men of her town would have the particular skills that belong to every step of the process. Her boys would be born to the sea and be at home in ships of every sort. Many of them would live their entire lives at sea.

Ships going back and forth to Europe, particularly to England, brought hints of life elsewhere. Old World customs and courtesies took root, and these made some of the difference between Portsmouth and her neighboring inland towns. There was a touch of aristocracy in her stately houses and in the manners of her people that owed something to Europe, something to the residence of royal governors during pre-Revolution years, something to the wealth of her merchants.

In the generation after Washington's visit, the wide mouth of the Piscataqua would be white with the skysails of the most beautiful ships man ever built, the clipper ships. They would sail the seven seas with more grace than any other ships in history. They would carry more and more of what

Portsmouth craftsmen made to the far corners of the globe and bring back more and more treasures from far places. We shall never see these queenly ships except in models or in an artist's imagination. Why should they have sailed the seas for one short generation only?

The answer—simply because the steamship was invented. Steamships were the triumph of another new day, and the glory of the clippers was ended. The skysails and the square-riggers would not come again. The trade of Portsmouth would be carried in faster, safer ships. Europe would be closer than ever before.

Then came the railroad, another triumph that nothing could stop. It changed not only the countryside, but also man's way of life. Rivers had been America's main traffic lanes since the beginning. Men had gone to Boston, to New York, and to points south by boat on rivers or on the ocean. For shorter distances they had gone by horseback trails. Coach travel had just begun to be regular and fairly comfortable. Now overland passengers went by train, which was faster and less infrequent. Many more could go. The railroad connected Portsmouth to the other New England towns by closer, firmer ties. Men and women who had never been farther than Dover or Exeter or Hampton now went to Boston, to New York, to Providence, and to many other places. Their view of America changed as it widened. The

LIGHTNING ROD *put up, according to tradition, by Benjamin Franklin on the Warner House. He was well known in Portsmouth and had had brief residence there.*

LEATHER BUCKETS *of water hanging above the stairs in the John Paul Jones House. All houses were so equipped in case of fire in early days. A mansion house, like this one, had elaborately decorated buckets.*

rails brought Portsmouth what her people needed. Prosperity came with this exchange. Not so many steamships came as before. Merchant ships now had a rival.

There have been many other ends and new beginnings. Today we give up the rails and ride on acres of cement made into four-lane highways, throughways, turnpikes, and slow up only to pay the toll. Perhaps we choose the sky above us when we go to Boston, to New York, to Providence, to Hartford, to Chicago, to Denver, to San Francisco, or to London and Paris. Transportation is, of course, only one change. Our way of life has survived many revolutions.

Portsmouth along with every other town and city of the land has had her share of all these changes. Her history shows that she has fitted herself into each new way of life as it has come. Her navy yard has made ships beyond any shipmaster's dream in the days of the *Ranger* and the

PORTIONS OF THE LOG WATER PIPE *from Portsmouth's first water system, 1799–1891. One of the first of its kind in the country. The water was brought from Warm Springs, at Oak Hill Farm (later called Fountain Head), two and a half miles to the Parade.*

America. She will keep on making what a modern navy requires, and always that will include something never made before.

Portsmouth is not a large city. In fact, in the whole state of New Hampshire there are hardly as many people as in a single moderately large American city—Pittsburgh, for example. Numbers are not as important as we sometimes think. Her plans for her own future take account of her situation as a seacoast town with a wide, deep harbor, islands that can be fortified to protect her, and a great river leading far into the land, too swift ever to freeze and with power to be harnessed for uses past counting. With all these natural advantages her new marine terminal promises to make her once more a great seaport. It is too early to predict, but the signs point to a day when the deep waters of the river Martin Pring discovered will be busier than ever before. If so, Portsmouth will take her place as she has done ever since the far-off days of Strawbery Banke. To read the history of this seaport town as it has been written for more than three hundred years, is to become acquainted with an American city that has been part of a new nation's experience in every chapter. In her beginnings and earlier years she is like every other early town in what she has lived through—discovery, hardship, danger, victory—and she is also different from them all, as each town must be different from all the others. Many things make it so.

Very soon, as Portsmouth plans, the summer visitors who come by many hundreds to see the noble mansions that survive from earlier days will also be able to walk over the small section of the present city that was once called Straw-bery Banke, restored in every detail to what it was three and a half centuries ago. This historic site around St. John's church, only a few minutes' walk from what is now Market Square, once called the Parade, will look as it did in Portsmouth's earliest chapter. Great House will be there, of course, just as Humphrey Chadbourne built it, with the storehouse, the blacksmith shop, the smaller houses of the first tenants close by. The old State House from which George Washington spoke will be there, the town pump, the whipping post, the cage in which those who smoked tobacco on Sunday were punished. Perhaps a few patches of wild strawberries can be encouraged to grow again. In imagination something of the life of the 1630s can be made clearer to us of another day.

But buildings, however correct in size, line, and material, are only shells. Footpaths are only lines on a map. The courage, the fortitude, the dream of better days ahead cannot be built of wood and stone. Continuing life on Strawbery Banke was possible because of something in the minds and hearts of these early pioneers that nothing can build or paint. They dreamed of a day when life there would be safer, more comfortable, and perhaps happier, and they worked for that day. As we perhaps walk the footpaths of a restored Strawbery Banke, as modern skill and imagination may achieve it, we salute these eighty men and women for what no picture can paint before our eyes. Their dreams, their determination, and their labor made possible this present city by the sea.

Index

Index

INDEX